DATE DUE			
AUG 2 4 70			
NOV 1 5 1988			
9/14/89			
GR B82			
GR B105			

170 IDEAL   PRINTED IN U.S.A.

This Is My
          Story,
This Is My
          Song

This Is My Story, This Is My Song

Jerome Hines

FLEMING H. REVELL COMPANY
OLD TAPPAN, NEW JERSEY

The Scripture quotations in this publication are taken from the *King James Version of the Bible,* unless otherwise identified.

*To the dear ones who have
sustained and comforted me always:
Mother, Father and Lucia, my wife.*

Preface

THIS ACCOUNT is not meant to be a literary masterpiece. In my busy life there is not enough time to sit down and polish up this manuscript even if I possessed the techniques and ability to do so. This tale could have been told to a professional writer, who might have made it much more acceptable by literary standards, but I wanted this true-life story to bear the simple ring of conviction and sincerity that can emerge only if it is recalled and told in the first person as it actually happened. The first chapter or two deal much with what Jerome Hines did and little with what God did. But this is essential, because an understanding of the background of my personality and problems is necessary to the understanding of how God has dealt with me since I found Him to be real.

Please don't make the mistake of thinking I am going to write a book about my belief in God. I don't believe in God—I know Him. There is a world of difference. And this book has been written to give an account of the truly miraculous things I have seen Him do. I will try not to preach at you, but to give you an eyewitness account of incidents I feel are too important to be left untold.

The average reader may never become involved in all

the improbable types of situations that are recounted here, but I hope he will be able to recognize in them a little bit of his own problems and failings and—hopefully—find some answers to help satisfy his life.

How does a skeptical, scientifically-trained mind come to recognize Jesus Christ as Saviour? Why do some people act as if they can talk with God and get answers? Do miracles exist? How can a man, at the pinnacle of Christian experience, cry out to God in desperation to kill him on the spot? And lastly, does God care for individuals? Does He provide for them and guide them in a personal way? My answer to this last question is an unequivocal "Yes!" And this book is meant to bring this reality home.

It begins as my story, but it ends another way.

Jerome Hines

Contents

This Is My
        Story,
This Is My
        Song

1.

Dead End

"HEY, GUYS, there's an XKE Jaguar," screamed Johnnie into my right ear.

I swerved the car back onto the road again, my head ringing like a gong and thought ruefully, "If any of my four sons ever becomes an opera singer it will surely be Johnnie, and he will be a heroic tenor to boot." His eight-year-old voice would sound fine in Yankee Stadium, but in the car it left my eardrum paralyzed.

Johnnie's Jag caused a big stir in the back seat. His brothers followed up his performance by trying to yell even louder. But as I turned to quiet them down I drew a glance from my wife which said, "Let them go, it's important to them."

Why was calling cars so important to a child? Yet I must have been like them once, becoming excited over little things and feeling misunderstood by my parents who could not seem to fathom the mystery and excitement in every breath of life. How do we adults so quickly lose our sense of wonder and the joy of little things? I tried to think back to what was important to me when I was their age. It was hard to remember, yet had it really been so long? My thoughts started to wander back, but a road sign brought me out of my reverie. There in the midst of the desert waste a large sign announced: Palm Springs. A wave of almost juvenile excitement swept over me. All of my life I had cherished a desire—an unfulfilled one—to visit this famous desert playground of the Hollywood stars. There it was that Rudolph Valentino. . . .

"But wait a moment," I thought, "Palm Springs?" I lifted my foot from the accelerator.

"What's up, Daddyo?" called my eleven-year-old, David.

"Just pipe down, fellas, I've got some thinking to do."

Lucia, my charming Italian wife, threw me an ominous look. I could tell from her expression she suspected what was wrong.

"Thees ees not San Diego," she said accusingly.

"Thank you, I can read the sign," I said with levity.

Her large Genovese eyes turned reproachful. "Thees ees not San Diego," she persisted.

"I've always wanted to see Palm Springs," I muttered lamely.

Again those Genovese eyes flashed. I knew what was coming and I braced myself. Then she asked the same question she has asked dozens of other times during our thirteen years of married life, "Where we are?"

"Palm Springs," I said innocently.

"You've done eet again. Why you always a stubborn to ask a direction?"

What could I say? I had done it again. My wife and I were due for a performance in San Diego in just a few hours, and I had already driven over sixty miles in the wrong direction. Grudgingly I turned off the main highway, and a few moments later I was facing a dead end. The dead silence in the car was even worse. I backed out, and with great distaste sought out the nearest gas station, humbling myself to ask for information, which I have always been loathe to do. Back on the road by which we had come, the stillness in the car gave me plenty of time for thinking.

"What a shame to be in Palm Springs for the first time in my life, and I can't even take five minutes to look around. And that dead end, that was the humiliating finale." I had to chuckle as I thought of the many times I had done the same thing in the past. Out of the corner of my eye I thought I caught a flicker of a smile on my wife's face.

"Well," I thought musingly, "everyone has their dead ends in one way or another, and many more serious than this."

This idea cheered me a little, in a perverse way, so I continued my line of thought. Dead ends—big ones and little ones—pop up unexpectedly in everyone's life all the time. If we back up, learn by our mistakes and try again in a new direction, our dead ends can be profitable experiences. But sometimes we are too stubborn or too lazy to back up and try again. We rationalize, claiming the dead end is not an error at all, but our intended goal. Many times a bright future has been ruined by the claim that life is empty, without meaning or purpose. Even worse, if a person in a position of leadership exalts and glorifies his own dead ends it can have disastrous results on society. How many founders of some of the world's greatest religious movements were trapped by the dead end of their own psychopathology, and, instead of admitting their error, they called their dead end, God? But people who live in glass houses. . . . There had been enough dead ends in my life too.

My thoughts turned to a dark, locked room in the basement of my New Jersey home. In its musty interior is one of the atrophied aspects of my life. Rows of beakers, flasks, chemicals and equipment, once bright and gleaming, now sit and gather dust. Six and a half years of studies, ending with degrees in chemistry, math and physics, are now symbolized by an empty and unused laboratory. My thoughts went further back, over thirty years.

My interest in chemistry began when I received a Chemcraft Set for my thirteenth birthday. One night as my family and I sat down to dinner I said, "I think I'd like to be a chemist."

"Now, you don't want to starve to death, do you?" my father rejoined. "All chemists starve."

"But I don't care," I continued doggedly; "I want to serve my fellow man."

"You can best start by serving your own family with a good living," my mother observed. "Charity begins at home."

During the main course I said, "But I really want to be a chemist."

"I've told you many times that Law would be a fine profession for you." Mother again! "And you'd better toe the mark in high school and get a 'B average' or you won't go to college at all."

That struck home. The year before, when I was in the ninth grade, my parents had been forced to hire a private tutor in arithmetic because I couldn't add, subtract, multiply or divide.

"You get your grades and you'll make a good lawyer."

"I want to be a chemist."

"Jerry, that's enough of that backtalk. You'll not be a chemist and that's final."

The discussion was finished but not my determination. A week later I alarmed the family by asking them to buy me some nitric acid.

"What do you want to do, blow up the house?"

"Acids don't blow up houses," I sighed condescendingly.

"No acids for a thirteen-year-old child!" was the flat answer. Day after day I persisted, and finally my distracted family decided I would have to have the advice of an experienced adult. Mother took me to a small, local chemical supply house. I stood in a trance gaping at a panorama of glassware and apparatus such as I had never dreamed possible. It was Utopia, Shangri-La, the Garden of Eden all wrapped up into one. I was hooked.

I began to scrounge and earn every last penny I could, and week after week a small but steady supply of equipment and chemicals began to pour into the house. After some haggling with my parents I acquired the premises of the back porch to house my expanding laboratory. Once I had built the shelves to harbor my chemicals, the first thing I bought to dedicate the new lab was a small bottle of uranium nitrate. Although I had no use for it and uranium was nothing more than a scientific curiosity with little practical value in those days, it was a rare and exotic chemical and slightly radioactive, which, of course, made it a very exciting acquisition. (That bottle of uranium nitrate still remains unopened on my dusty laboratory shelf in the basement of our home in New Jersey. In a sense it is a symbol of this particular dead end in my life—chemistry.)

When I bought that little brown bottle its exotic contents symbolized a deep longing that I couldn't define or explain, a longing that was to grow fiercer and more implacable as the years passed. In that bottle was a mystery; just as there is a mystery to all of life. I was compelled to probe and seek out all the answers; little knowing that the answers would lead only to more questions with the mystery becoming more intangible and perhaps forever unknowable.

As a child I had always been a dreamer rather than a doer. I was extremely tall and painfully thin—the continual target of abuse from larger bullies. I began to withdraw into a dream world of abstraction—chemistry seemed to fill my needs. Sports didn't interest me, only textbooks. With girls I made no headway; I was too shy and ungainly.

As I entered my last year of high school, my parents finally relented and granted my wish to enter college the next year as a chemistry major. But as time passed my mother's concern for my withdrawn and introverted nature deepened. One day she confided her concern to a neighbor, Mrs. Catherine Cotter, who was a registered nurse.

Mrs. Cotter answered, "Why don't you send him out to Alhambra with my daughter to take singing lessons? Perhaps studying voice with the possibility of performing in public will bring out his personality and extrovert him somewhat."

When my mother suggested singing lessons to me, nothing could have been farther from my mind. I was not averse to the idea, but the only musical background I had had was two and a half years of intermittent piano lessons, and during my junior high school days I had been kicked out of the Glee Club because I couldn't carry a tune! (Seemingly nobody in my family was musical, although I did find out years later that my great grandfather, Bill Reynolds, whom I closely resembled, had been a minstrel singer.)

Eventually I went to Alhambra with my mother, Mrs. Cotter and her daughter. I met tall, kindly, white-haired Lucy McCullough—"Aunt Lucy" to all of her friends. She asked me to sing something, and I strode to the piano and sang the song, popular at that time, "Empty Saddles." I crooned it an octave lower than it was written, and I could hardly be heard across the room. Then we did a few scales and Aunt Lucy remarked, "He does seem to have a nice quality to his voice, so come back next week and we'll start to work."

During the first lesson, Aunt Lucy encouraged me to let my voice out a bit, and to stop imitating Bing Crosby.

"It looks as if we've found something here," she said, with enthusiasm. After several lessons she began to hint that I might have operatic talent. Not trusting her own judgment, she took me to her old teacher, Roland Paul, and had me sing for him. He was extremely enthusiastic and encouraged me to think seriously of opera.

But to leave chemistry would be unthinkable! I began to wonder if I could successfully combine my two careers —singing and chemistry. Two months later Aunt Lucy announced to me that she was no longer going to teach me. I was thunderstruck, and asked her why.

"Jerry, I'm not qualified to teach a person with a voice like yours. You need someone who can train you for the opera stage. Go find yourself a teacher who can do justice to your voice," she said.

Within a short time my mother had investigated the best teachers in town and approached Maestro Gennaro Curci. In addition to having been a fine basso cantante with an extensive career behind him, he was the brother-in-law and vocal coach of the famous coloratura, Galli-Curci.

"Madam, I don't teach children," the Maestro said firmly.

"This is the biggest child you've ever seen," she answered. (She should have said the "tallest" because although my height was 6' 6", I weighed only 150 pounds.)

Maestro Curci reluctantly agreed to hear me. He had never accepted a male pupil under the age of eighteen, but after my audition he agreed to give me two lessons a week. I immediately began my lessons and before long this wise, practical, artistic and sensitive man, who had abandoned his career to devote himself full-time to the coaching and training of his famous sister-in-law, began to place his own unfulfilled ambitions upon my shoulders. A relationship began to grow between us, almost as deep as that of father and son.

Meanwhile, with my parents' blessing I went to the University of California at Los Angeles to study chemistry. As my studies progressed I began taking extra courses by examination, in addition to my regular curriculum, which enabled me to pick up enough extra credits to acquire a double major. And what was the extra subject? Mathematics! The very subject in which I had done so poorly in junior high. It had now taken a place of immense importance in my studies because of its necessity in science, and I was growing to enjoy it more than any of my other academic pursuits.

In my second year of college I landed my first professional singing job, as Bill Bobstay in *HMS Pinafore,* during the spring season of Edwin Lester's Los Angeles Civic

Light Opera Company, with performances both in San Francisco and Los Angeles. In order to get the contract I had to make one concession. The spelling of my last name had to be changed from Heinz to Hines, because Lester didn't want my name associated with the Heinz of pickle fame (57 varieties) who was some sort of a distant relation to my father. Singing in *Pinafore* was a great thrill to me because I was to perform with John Charles Thomas, the great baritone, and I learned much by listening night after night to his flawless vocal production.

Only two months later Maestro Curci had me sing for Gaetano Merola, General Manager of the San Francisco Opera Company, and I had my first opera contract with a major opera company at the tender age of eighteen. Three months later I debuted as Monterone in *Rigoletto* with such greats of that generation as Lawrence Tibbett and Lily Pons. Debuting with me was Jan Peerce, who, as a result of his triumphant performances, received his first contract with the Metropolitan Opera.

Because of these performances I lost a year at the university, but I returned to my studies in science because I had many years of vocal study ahead of me before I could make it a full-time career. Soon thereafter World War II broke out and I was deferred as a student preparing for an industry essential to the war effort.

At the end of my eighteenth year I met a man who had a great influence on my career as a singing actor. One of the few true geniuses I have met in my life, Vladimir Rosing was a Russian Jew from Leningrad. I met Val when I auditioned successfully for an opera company he was starting in Los Angeles. Over more than twenty-four years I had the occasion to study the characterization of all my major roles with him. He had more to do with the growth of my formative years as a singer than anyone except Maestro Curci himself. Working with these two brilliant artists was going to serve in launching me into a very early career, with excellent preparation.

Under Maestro Curci's tutelage I began to learn Italian and French, and by the age of twenty I knew twenty operas in their original languages. Working with these great men was a direct act of God, and I will ever be appreciative and grateful for what they did. Surely without them, and the faithfulness of my parents, I would not be enjoying the career I have now. (In my later years at the Metropolitan Opera my good fortune was to continue under the expert guidance of Samuel Margolis, who took over my vocal training in New York. Since that time I have worked exclusively with that talented man for years.)

During my nineteenth year another factor entered my life—I acquired my first regular church membership. A Methodist Church pastored by Reverend John Engle in Hollywood had a very active youth program, and I began to attend regularly. Very soon I was involved in all phases of church activities, often singing solos, and on many occasions trying out religious songs I had composed, including a "Lord's Prayer" which I wrote when I was twenty. Pastor Engle was especially interested in young people and endeavored to encourage their thinking. As a result of many spiritual bull sessions with the Pastor I began to get more involved in the more serious aspects of the church; even to the point where I was given the task of conducting an entire Good Friday service, since I had repeatedly objected to the church ritual, and especially the tuneless singing of the choir.

I had many ideas which in my naïvete I considered avante-garde. I used to wrangle over them with Pastor Engle to all hours of the night. Finally he invited me to try my views out on the congregation in a sermonette, and several Sundays later I found myself in the pulpit delivering a dissertation on prayer.

"God does not answer prayer," I said. "He is not a personal deity who busies himself with the mundane affairs of two billion individuals. To quote Benjamin Franklin, 'God helps those that help themselves.' Do not expect God to wait upon you with miracles. The only value of prayer is in drawing close enough to that cosmic force called 'God' so that you may be inspired to do a better job."

I reasoned that, "God in His foreknowledge had included in this universe all that was necessary to its eventual perfection from the first moment of its creation, and He is not about to disturb its scientifically ordered perfection by dabbling with it throughout the course of history."

In my short twenty-one years of life I had never witnessed a miracle, nor had I ever had a prayer answered. In all honesty I was giving testimony to what I had seen, or rather what I had not seen. I thought my sermon was bold and challenging. Had I been more perceptive I would have realized that I had ignited no great stir of controversy in the congregation. I had merely presented the common garden-variety type of religious belief held by the majority of people everywhere. They too had heard of miracles, but had never seen one. They too had prayed to an infinite, unknowable God and had received no answers. I, like they, had invented a religion of convenience that permitted me to continue in my own self-centered way of life undisturbed. I had reached a dead end and called it God; a god created in my own image, a god who was the product of my flimsy human logic, a god that had no relationship to Eternal Truth whatsoever.

For the time this was all the God I needed. I had a voice and talent and was driven by worldly ambitions. I was going places fast, and the whole world lay before me. I had no family responsibilities, and I surely felt I was master of my own fate. I knew as soon as the war ended I was practically assured of a successful operatic career. I had no need of a personal God or answered prayer. I felt I was sufficient unto myself, and instead of thinking of what God needed to do for me, I was thinking of what I was going to do for Him.

2.

Conviction

I RECEIVED my bachelor's degree, with a double major in chemistry and math and went on to complete all of the requirements for my master's degree in chemistry, except for the thesis.

The years that I spent at UCLA were busy ones, for during that time I continued taking eight to twelve private voice and coaching lessons with the maestro each week. I also began work as a chemist on the night shift of Union Oil Company of California, and at the behest of the head of the Physics Department of UCLA, I changed my major to Physics, attending classes during the day. Only the vigor of youth and determination helped me survive the strain of eight hours of night shift, several hours of classes at UCLA and lessons with Maestra Curci—all mixed generously with hours of driving to and fro.

During my last year and a half at UCLA I began practicing hypnosis under the guidance of a professor of psychology, which fitted well into my amateur delvings into psychiatry. But, as in all my other endeavors, I did not find in hypnosis that mysterious something for which I was searching. Was it not that beautiful "fleeting moment"

I was seeking? That "fleeting moment" that relentlessly drove Goethe's Faust to endless searching. Does it not drive all mankind?

During the last war years I managed to slip away for short periods to perform in opera around the country. The management of the Metropolitan Opera Company began to hear of me, but I could not leave my essential war job as an oil chemist.

Then World War II came to an end. I was now free to pursue my operatic career. Val Rosing, returning from a trip to New York, told me the Met had expressed interest in hearing me sing. I sent a telegram to Edward Johnson, general manager of the Opera House, saying that I could be in New York in two months, after finishing some engagements in New Orleans. An immediate reply fixed the date of my audition.

Maestro Curci decided he would come too, at his own expense, to see that everything went well. I auditioned excerpts from *Faust* and *Boris Godunov*, and the next morning was offered a contract. I signed my first Met contract at the age of twenty-four. I was the youngest member of the Met at that time, and Edward Johnson took great pride in introducing me to everyone as his baby.

In November of 1946 I debuted at the Met, playing the supporting role of the frontier guard, in *Boris Godunov*. Ezio Pinza sang the title role. After this inauspicious start, my second performance was as Mephistopheles in *Faust,* a big responsibility for one so young. (Fortunately I had already sung the role seventeen times before joining the Met.) These two operas I repeated throughout the season, meanwhile understudying another two dozen roles.

During my first season Mr. Johnson came to me after a *Faust* performance and informed me that I had just won the coveted Caruso Award of $1000, given to the outstanding young Met singer of the year.

During my second year at the Met I established myself thoroughly by singing eleven operas. By the end of the fourth year at the Met I had sung well over twenty roles and had begun to think of Europe to expand my horizons.

One day Mr. Johnson called me into his office and asked about my plans for the summer. I told him I intended to go to Europe, buy a bicycle and tour for about two months.

"Perhaps I can help you buy that bicycle," he observed, and within a week told me I had received the annual Bliss award of $1000.

That summer of 1950 was exciting in many ways! In addition to the European trip I sang the first of many performances with the Firestone Hour on television and did Mephistopheles in *Faust* three times in the Hollywood Bowl. During the rehearsals for *Faust* a significant incident occurred, which began a chain of events that was to alter the entire course of my life.

During a rehearsal break, two men introduced themselves as the general manager and business manager for the Pilgrimage Bowl. (The Pilgrimage Bowl was located in the Hollywood hills directly across the highway from

the Hollywood Bowl, was under the same general management, and had been built for the presentation of an annual pilgrimage play, which had run for more than twenty
years with Nelson Leigh playing the part of Christ.)

These two gentlemen asked me if I knew anyone who
would be willing to write some background music for the
finale of their passion play. The passion play was on its
last legs, and they felt the production needed a little shot
in the arm, they told me. I said I would discuss it with
Albert Hay Malotte, a close friend of mine, who had
written the world-famous musical setting of the Lord's
Prayer.

The next week I made the proposal to Malotte, but he
was not interested.

Then I said, "Albert, I've been trying to get you to
write an opera ever since I met you, and it's just occurred
to me that no one has ever written the 'Life of Christ'
as an opera. Why don't you write an operatic passion
play?"

No amount of persuasion could budge him, but the
idea stayed in my mind. Somewhat of an amateur composer myself, I toyed with the idea of writing an operatic
passion play on my own. In my spare time I planned a
libretto and put some music to the Luke version of the
Sermon on the Mount. The work was painfully slow at
first because I worked sporadically and had no formal
training in music. But one important factor was in evi-
dence: In preparing the libretto I was beginning to read
the Bible, particularly the New Testament, leaning heav-

ily on the book of John. I didn't understand much of
what I was reading, but it was having a profound effect,
unbeknownst to me, and I was due soon for a major
spiritual upheaval.

The summer of 1950 also marked the end of Edward
Johnson's long term as general manager of the Metropolitan. I was happy to find my name on the first pub-
lished list of singers to be rehired for the next season,
and my first year under Rudolf Bing (Johnson's succes-
sor) went quite well.

Then an all-important incident occurred. In the summer of 1951 I went to Cincinnati to sing *Faust* and met
a young tenor who had come to Ohio to study voice with
one of the conductors there.

One day as he and I sat in the lobby of the Alms Hotel
he said, "Jerome, today you are going to meet the most
beautiful woman in the world."

I raised my eyebrows skeptically.

"I am madly in love with her, but she does not know
I exist."

Suddenly his face lit up, and he squeezed my arm
warningly. I saw a petite, red-haired Italian girl coming
our way. He mustered all his courage and called, *Signorina Evangelista venga qui, per favore.*" "Miss Lucia
Evangelista," he whispered to me, "doesn't speak too
much English."

His heart's desire strolled in our direction with a dif-
fident, almost bored, expression and was introduced to

me. With a minimum of social amenities she asked to be excused and promptly left. My smitten friend stood looking after her in a trance. A tap on the shoulder brought him back to the lobby of the Alms Hotel.

"Well, what do you think?" he asked.

"I'm sorry, buddy, she's not my type." I couldn't have startled him more if I'd said Beethoven was a bum. No amount of arguing on his part could convince me otherwise.

"But she's the dream girl of Cincinnati. You should hear her Violetta, her Mimi."

"Sorry, buddy, I don't date girls to hear them sing, I get enough of that on the stage. She's just not my type."

He wrote me off as a lost cause. The following day I had a free evening so I began to prowl about the company to find a date for dinner and a movie. A ballerina had caught my eye during rehearsals and I made my pitch. Sorry, she was booked up. Next I tried a soprano I knew; she was singing that night: "Didn't you know?" Again and again I tried, until I had practically gone through the entire company. When I was about to give up, Miss Evangelista happened by.

"Oh Signorina, would you care to have supper with me and see a movie tonight?" A slight smirk on her face made me realize she had probably heard of my well-known philandering.

"Ima sorry," she said. "Tomorrow night I sing performances. So tonight I go early to bed."

"Well . . . how about supper, then?"

"Va bena," she said reluctantly. "What time?"

We made the arrangements unenthusiastically and parted. At five she called my room to cancel the appointment, but I wasn't in, so we went out just the same. By the time supper was over it was a case of love at second sight.

A week later, as I was waiting at the stage door for Miss Evangelista—who was now Lucia to me—my tenor friend Tish walked by. News travels fast in an opera company.

"Not your type," he purred sarcastically. "Ha!"

Day by day the romance grew more serious and before long, back in New York, my list of regular dates had dwindled to one solitary Lucia Evangelista. The following spring I proposed, and one evening in the summer of 1952 I flew back to Cincinnati to claim my bride.

It was eight o'clock when I climbed off the plane. Lucia and my good friend Jim Sardos were on hand to meet me. Jim was a great opera lover who had begun as a standee at the Met. He and I had become inseparable, and now he had flown to Cincinnati to be with us. Lucia and I had planned to apply for a license at once and then wait the required three days, but Lucia had good news:

"Darleeng," she cried excitedly, "we can get marry tonight. I find a nice lady doctor, and she ees waiting to testa you blood and she drives to Indiana tonight, and we are marry."

Within a few minutes the bags were in a rented car, and we three were headed for the office of Dr. Aurelia

McIntyre, in mid-town Cincinnati. I was adjusting myself
to the thought of losing my last three days of freedom
when Lucia said, "Jerry, thees ees your las' chance to back-
ing out before marry."

I slammed on the brakes and threw open my door, as if
to jump out while the car was still in motion. Jim threw
open his door and *did* jump. I looked in open-mouthed
amazement as he disappeared. The car was still moving
at about twenty-five or thirty miles an hour. Fortunately,
Jim is well-nigh indestructible, and a few moments after
I stopped the car he hobbled up with nothing more than
a torn jacket and a bruise or two to show.

"I thought you had stopped the car," he groaned.

"Idiot!"

We got under way again and soon arrived at the doctor's
office. Dr. McIntyre and her husband, one of the leading
psychiatrists in Cincinnati, drove us to Lawrenceburg,
Indiana, where we were to be married by a Justice of the
Peace. (The reason for the hurry was that at ten the
next morning Lucia had a dress rehearsal of *La Boheme*
and two performances in the following four days, after
which I had to leave for my second trip to Europe, while
Lucia remained in Cincinnati to sing.)

At 1:30 A.M. July 23, 1952, we stood before a Justice
of the Peace. When he said to Lucia, "Repeat after
me . . ." she whispered to me, "I can't. He talksa too
fast."

"Quiet. Do as he says."

The Justice began to intone, "I, Lucia Evangelista, take

thee, Jerome Hines, to be my lawful wedded husband. . . ."

She dutifully answered, "I, Lucia Evangelista, take dee, Jerome Hines, to be my *awful* wedded husband. . . ."

Jim Sardos' uncontrolled hysterics almost disrupted the service, but somehow we managed to tie the knot.

What followed immediately after has been typical of our lives ever since. At ten the following morning Lucia was on stage rehearsing *La Boheme*. That evening she performed *La Traviata,* and did *Boheme* the next night. The following day we left for New York where we spent a one day honeymoon, and I left for Europe and Lucia flew back to Cincinnati for *Carmen*. Despite such obstacles our marriage got off to a happy start, and I soon began to wonder why I had stayed a bachelor so long.

As the next year passed I seemed to have all a young man could want. I had waited to marry until my career was firmly established, I had found the one and only girl in the world for me, and now, to top it off we found we were approaching the proud responsibility of parenthood. Surely mine was a full life. But some people never seem to be satisfied with anything and I seemed to be definitely one of those.

I recall one night when my wife awoke at 4:00 A.M. and found me sitting up in bed wide awake and pensive.

"Whatsa wrong? Why you don' sleep?"

"I don't know, dear," I answered. "There's always been something in my life that. . . . Well, I just can't explain it. It seems to be something I'm looking for and can never find. It's like an itch I can't scratch, but it's in the spirit. Yes, that's it, it's like a spiritual unrest or wander-lust, a sense of unfulfilled destiny. It's a strange and sad loneliness, and yet it's not that either. I don't know, I can't explain it."

"You crazy?" my wife asked delicately.

"Maybe," I said, quietly smiling. "I only know that I've always been cursed with this thing. I suppose I'll go through my whole life just looking and never finding. Maybe what I'm looking for doesn't even exist."

"You crazee all right. Good night."

I lay in bed still sleepless and filled with longing and wonderment. Why had I plunged so hard into science, when a career in opera was already assured? I was search-ing, of course! Why the delving into psychiatry, compos-ing, hypnotism and all the rest? I was searching desper-ately for something that eternally eluded me. Every en-deavor led to a dead end. (There was that word again.) Was my entire life to terminate in a dead end? I knew then that success in my profession and a happy home life would still be empty without this unknown urge being fulfilled. The mystery deepened and my restlessness grew.

Meanwhile my wife and I began to build our family life in Manhattan. We rented a large apartment up on 67th Street and Broadway and of course our habitual guest for supper was Jim Sardos, who was a constant source of merriment and humor. My wife seriously began to wonder whether she had married Jerome Hines or both Jerome Hines and Jim Sardos!

Since Jim shared my love of chemistry, he proposed one day that we build a laboratory. We discovered that the Lincoln Center Building was most suitable so we rented a large room there. Within a short time, Jim and Lucia and I were busy at work painting the walls, laying a tile floor and building all sorts of tables and sinks for a chemistry laboratory. After two months we completed a very satisfactory arrangement and moved in about 80 percent of my total lab, which I had brought back from California in a station wagon.

Lucia meanwhile was busying herself with domestic affairs. Soon she and I began to prepare for our first Christmas together. She had never had presents or a tree in Italy, and as we shopped together, it was a joy to watch her; she was like a child in wonderland—buying gifts, a tree, tinsel and Christmas balls. In her enthusiasm she overdid, and one day she had unpleasant symptoms.

The doctor said she was in danger of losing her baby and within an hour my wife was at Flower and Fifth Avenue Hospital. For about two days they fought to save the child, but two hours after his birth, a nurse came to tell me that the baby had expired.

When the doctor broke the news to my wife, he asked for permission to perform an autopsy to see if he could determine the cause of the premature birth. After the autopsy he told us that nothing had been wrong with the baby.

"The trouble, Mrs. Hines, I'm afraid is with you. With

your medical history, it is very possible that you will not be able to bear a child to full term."

"You mean that I can't have babies? A child of my own?"

"That remains to be seen. From your case history, it looks doubtful; however, I suggest that you try again. And please, during your next pregnancy, be very careful: Don't do any traveling, don't do *anything* that would bring on a premature birth again."

This news was, of course, a great blow to both of us. For the next few months, Lucia couldn't even look at a child without bursting into tears and becoming hysterical.

Before long we discovered that my wife was pregnant again. And now her panic began. She was afraid that she couldn't have this child either. She would say to me, "You marry the wrong girl, I'm a failure as a wife, I'm a failure as a woman—you shoulda marry someone else." Her fears grew daily as her pregnancy progressed.

Meanwhile another source of trouble had begun to brew —this time in my career. It had been announced that the Metropolitan Opera would do *Boris Godunov* in the 1952-3 season. Since performing the title role of Boris is the great dream of all operatic bassos, I went right to the management and asked how many performances I was to have. I had never sung Boris and had long anticipated doing it. I was shocked almost to tears, when I was told that I was not to sing the role. I was too young, had never done the opera in another theater, and the Metropolitan was not a conservatory for untried ventures. Then, to rub salt into the wound, I was forced to sing the secondary role of Pimen in *Boris* instead of the title role. I had never felt so humiliated.

When the time came for me to perform the role I was in a dreadful state of mind. After the second performance, I was so upset that when I went home that night I could not sleep. About three o'clock in the morning my wife woke up and saw me sitting up in bed. She said, "What in earth you sit up in bed for now?"

I said, "I've just decided that if I don't do the title role in *Boris* next season at the Met, I'm going to quit and go to Europe."

"Suppose Mr. Bing saya no? You mean you would really leave?"

"Yes I would. I will go to Europe and make myself a career there." I was firm and determined.

Lucia realized my disturbed state and came out with a profound statement. "I just realize, your career is a most important thing to you in alla your life. It mean more to you than I do."

I turned to her quickly, to try to say to her "No, it's not true," but my tongue would not move, because deep in my heart I knew it was so. I knew that before all things in the world, my career came first. It was a shock to realize that my career came even before my family life and my own wife—but it was a reality.

The next morning I called my lawyer and told him that if I did not sing Boris at the Metropolitan Opera

House the following season I would leave the theater, and that he was to deliver this ultimatum to Mr. Bing. I already knew that Mr. Bing was not a man accustomed to yielding to ultimatums, from the cases of Lawrence Melchior and Helen Traubel, and I fully expected to be told to pack my bags and leave for Europe, but I knew that I could not continue with the situation as it was. A day or two later, my lawyer, Mr. Gins, called me back and said, "Mr. Bing will give you one performance as Boris next season, but he is not very happy about it." But I was! I soon discovered that Mr. Bing had an extra reason for being unhappy about me singing Boris; he was importing a famous bass from Italy to sing the role, which brought the total number of singers doing the role that season to four, if I were included. One opera house just doesn't have four people singing the same leading role during one season! Furthermore, the bass coming from Italy had the reputation of being the greatest Boris in the world.

Within a day or two I said to a good friend of mine, who was staging the opera for Mr. Bing, "Well I won my fight, I'm going to sing Boris next season. I'll be performing it with you. Isn't that great?"

"What do you mean great? After all, the Met is bringing this new bass from Italy to do Boris, and he is acclaimed as the greatest Boris in the world. And two of your other colleagues have already done it successfully last season. You will be absolutely lost in the shuffle when you do it. It's very bad timing. If you have any sense at all, you will go back to Mr. Bing and say, 'I have chosen the wrong time—I am not ready to do the part and would prefer to wait another year or two before I perform it.' "

"You're a fine friend, you are," I complained.

"No, honestly, I am really being a good friend to give you this advice. You've chosen the wrong time to do Boris; when this other fellow comes in, he's going to be an enormous success and you won't even be remembered."

I left the theater discouraged and sour. I was beginning to wonder if it was worth all the trouble. Was I wrong? Should I wait for another season or two before doing Boris? All the odds were against me, and my doubts began to grow.

Meanwhile I had plenty of other things to be happy about. My wife was pregnant again, and I had been offered a contract to sing *Don Giovanni* in Munich, Germany. From there I was to fly to South America to perform the opera, *Don Carlos*. Next I was to fly to New York and do another Firestone television show and then back across the ocean to sing the part of Nick Shadow in *Rake's Progress*, by Stravinsky, at the Edinburgh Festival. But this good news was also a cause for anxiety. It meant a considerable amount of air travel and my wife of course wanted to accompany me in spite of her "delicate condition," as the Italians call it. She pointed out that I would be gone for over three months and that she would be sitting in New York all by herself. She didn't speak much English and she had no friends there other than Jim

Sardos. She was rapidly approaching a condition of complete panic over her pregnancy. After much pleading on her part I decided to let her accompany me on the trip.

Unbeknownst to me, God was beginning to influence my life by pressures and situations that were to force me into a whole new world of Christian experience. My recent problems had badly shaken my self-confidence and also I had been doing more and more reading in the Bible, particularly in the New Testament. I didn't realize the deep effect all this was beginning to have on me.

As the Metropolitan season came to an end we began packing for the Met tour. It would be an endless round of performances, train trips, receptions and parties, and perhaps too strenuous for Lucia.

After the tour we left the company and flew to Florence, Alabama, for a recital. Following the concert, Lucia and I went to bed about two. We were to arise early in the morning because we had to make a long flight to Astoria, Oregon, where I was to do another recital.

During the night I had a most unusual dream—a dream that was to be the first of many experiences that were destined to alter my life.

3.

Try Me

IN MY DREAM I was lying on the grassy slope of a hillside. It was a beautiful spring day with a blue sky and big white clouds rushing by. Lying open beside me on the ground was a black book. The shadows from the clouds overhead were racing over the mountainside and closing in about me. They pressed in closer and narrowed down upon the book that was lying next to me. I looked closer and saw that a ray of sunlight was shining and burning bright as fire on two lines in the open book. I knew I was supposed to read these lines and I leaned over to scan them. As I read the words I heard a voice like thunder echoing them from heaven. It said, "This is my beloved Son in whom I am well pleased." Until that moment I believed that all people were God's children and surely felt I was. But in the dream, my feeling was reversed. I knew those words I had just read spoke of Jesus and that they came from the New Testament—one of the four gospels. (I had been reading enough of the Bible lately to know that much.) As I pondered on Jesus being the Son of God, an alien thought transfixed my heart like an arrow. Suddenly I knew that *I* was not a son of God. I knew that

I did not belong to Him and there was nothing I could do about it through my own efforts. I felt a horrible crushing sensation and then the scene changed and I was infinitely high in the heavens looking down at Jerome Hines on that hillside. But I was looking down at him *through the eyes of God.* I saw myself as God saw me.

I saw Jerome Hines there as a grain of dust—he was nothing. And the shock of seeing myself by the eyes of God and by the standards of God was an experience so crushing and horrifying that I would never wish it upon any living being. I felt as though I had been completely demolished, pulverized.

Then I was back on the hillside so devastated that I began to cry out like a lost soul. The emotion of the dream became intolerable and I wrenched awake, perspiring and shocked. But I lay there in the dark unable to move for ten minutes. I could not shake off that horrible lost feeling. Finally I forced myself to turn on the light to get a sense of proper perspective.

My wife sat up and said, "What'sa matter?"

I said, "Dear, I've had a very strange dream, let me tell you about it." When I finished relating my dream, I broke into tears. Lucia held me in her arms as though I were a child and for almost a half hour I wept bitterly. Finally having cried myself out I slunk to my bed and went fitfully to sleep. The next morning I awoke feeling rather foolish. And my wife and I tacitly tried to forget the whole situation. But everywhere I was to go in the next few months the depression of that lost feeling would be there to dog my footsteps.

Our summer travels took us to Europe and, after singing in Munich, we visited Lucia's family in northern Italy. We stopped in Rome and revisited Saint Peter's Cathedral at Vatican City, and I was again (as I had been on my solo trip three years before) smitten by the beauty and grandeur.

As we walked out of the building and down the wide, worn steps to the piazza I watched a white-bearded old priest trudge wearily to the top—he seemed almost too old and tired to make it. Thoughts flitted through my mind: Although the Catholic church was not my church, their thinking not my thinking, the fact remained that over the centuries multitudes of men had trod these steps seeking to serve God in their own ways.

"What have I done to serve God—what part have I with Him?" I reflected. And the same nightmarish, lost sensation I had experienced in my dreams in Alabama seized me. It persisted until we left Rome for Buenos Aires twenty-four hours later.

When we arrived in Argentina the weather was below freezing, and I immediately caught a cold. My condition was aggravated even more by the heavily polluted air (all the private homes and apartments were heated by stoves that burned gasoline) and I came down with a series of crippling asthmatic attacks. For my entire month in that city, every night was an agony of choking and fighting for breath.

Throughout my teens and twenties in Los Angeles I had been afflicted by hay fever and asthma, caused primarily by the smog, but in the East I had had no difficulty. Now it had returned to plague me at a most important time:

I was performing Philip the Second in *Don Carlos,* one of the most important roles in my repertoire, in one of the most important theaters in the world. To add to the problem, Argentina under Peron was rabidly anti-American. I was met with outright hostility, by many people in the city, prior to my performances. Also, it was inconceivable to the Argentine public that a North American should sing Philip in this classic Verdi opera. All I needed was asthma!

One doctor finally brought me some relief in the form of just plain adrenalin. I had adrenalin pills and an adrenalin solution in which I soaked a little wad of cotton and put the wad under my tongue for quick relief. The trouble was that when I took the adrenalin to cure my attack, I couldn't sleep because the adrenalin stimulated me and kept me awake. Somehow I managed to make a successful debut at the Teatro Colon which insured many years of return engagements.

From Argentina we flew home to New York, did a Firestone show and then left immediately for England, where Lucia and I went to live in the country near the little town of Kent, while I was preparing to do *Rake's Progress* in Edinburgh. There must have been something in that country air to which I was terribly allergic, because my already irritated bronchial tubes began again to give me a lot of trouble. Every night, around two, I would wake up gasping for breath and would remain so until about eight o'clock, when I had to drag myself out to rehearsals. The lack of sleep began to affect my physical condition.

The little town of Kent is a very quiet place. We rehearsed only in the daytime and our evenings were free, but there was absolutely nothing to do after supper. Fortunately, the large home in which we had rented a room had a piano on the main floor. Evening after evening I sat at the piano and composed a little more music for my opera on the life of Jesus. Almost four years had passed since I had begun and I had written a grand total of fourteen pages. Obviously I had not been working at the project very seriously. Now with plenty of spare time in which to work, my composing began to progress.

I had begun to write the Sermon on the Mount as my first scene and I was worried particularly about one segment. It was the famous quotation, "Love your enemies, bless them that curse you, do good to them that hate you and pray for them which despitefully use you" (Matthew 5:44). This part of the gospel seemed to me to be the whole crux of Christianity. I dreaded writing the music for it because I felt that I would be inadequate. As the evenings passed I finally arrived in my libretto at just that point.

As I looked at Jesus' words I knew that I could not put them to music. Richard Wagner himself, who certainly would have been a man musically and technically equipped to write such a work, had balked at writing an opera on the life of Christ although he contemplated it for his entire life. The great Berlioz had considered writing an opera on the life of Christ and yet had put it off and had died prematurely before he was able to start. How could *I* put those words to music? Who was I to write an opera about Him of whom I knew nothing and with whom I had no dealings? The audacity of it! I had no qualifications other than a small ability for writing melodies and an over-inflated ego. I had never studied music formally; I knew nothing of harmony, counterpoint or orchestration; yet I had a burning desire to do this work. I also felt the need for a new theme at this point, a theme representing the Holy Spirit. But how could *I* write it?

"God, I can't. I can't do it. God, write this music for me. Of myself I cannot. I am not worthy to even speak Thy holy words, let alone put them to music. God, please write it for me."

A sure and warm feeling came over me. I put my hands on the keyboard and the music I could not write soon flowed—every note seemed just right for those glorious words.

"Dear, I want you to hear what I just wrote. Come!" I called to Lucia.

When I finished playing and singing I looked over at my wife—she was crying like a baby.

"What is it? What is wrong, dear?"

"Darling," she said, "I can't help eet. That music. I've heard all the music you write, but you never wrote music like that. It's so beautiful I had to cry."

"I couldn't put music to these words, but I prayed and

asked God to do it for me, and—well I feel that He did."

That night I lay awake thinking of how strange and powerful had been His presence—and so close—as if He were a personal God and one could know Him and be aware of Him. It was almost as if God Himself had guided my hands to write that music. If this were to happen again perhaps I could write an opera.

In a rare moment of self-honesty I admitted to myself that I was not composing an opera; I was only dabbling around and creating a conversation piece. I didn't seriously believe I would ever complete and perform the entire work. Who was I kidding but myself?

But if I really worked seriously, how long would it take for me to finish an opera? I figured nine years. I would then be about forty years old and should be in the prime of my vocal and histrionic abilities as a singer. I would have to be, to tackle the enormous job of singing the part of Jesus Christ. Then I could begin to produce and perform this work as my service to God.

"God," I whispered, "if I write this work and perform it to Your glory, will you make it your work too? Will you write it for me as you did tonight?"

A thought hit me like a lightning bolt: *"I will."*

I felt as if God had answered me in my heart. Thrilled by this I wondered what it would be like to do such a work.

Would this really satisfy me? I wondered. Had I actually come upon the answer to thirty years of searching? Was that which I had sought so long, God Himself? Had

I been wrong all the time? Was He truly a personal, knowable God? That thought cut through me like a sword. Was it possible that an omnipotent God could be aware of one Jerome Hines—even, possibly, concerned for him?

"But," I whispered again, "how do I know you are God? I can't write this work without you, yet how do I know I'm not just talking to myself? If you are God, prove it! Do a miracle like—like. . . ." Then I thought of my asthma attacks. "All right, if you are God, see that I don't have an asthma attack tonight."

The lightning bolt hit me again! *"Try me!"*

My mind churned before the horizons that were opening up before me, and it was a while before I dozed off. About four in the morning I awoke lying on my right side. I thought a moment—how long had it been since I had slept this long without an attack of asthma?

Could it mean . . . ? No! The rational processes of a scientifically trained mind began to creep in. "It's just coincidence that the attacks ended tonight, and you call it God." I turned over in bed, and I began to wheeze immediately.

"Oh —— it," I muttered. The profanity had no sooner left my lips than the lightning bolt struck again.

"Now you have seen. Turn back on your right side and don't move."

I lay motionless for a moment, and I felt the hair prickling on the back of my neck. Then I relaxed a little— the situation was certainly eerie, but . . . well, what had I to lose? I turned over. In all my years of experience

with asthma I had never had an attack recede spontane-
ously. It was ridiculous to think that by turning onto my
right side the attack would stop! Well, ridiculous or not it
did stop.

Then the inner voice spoke again, *"Now stay on your
right side and go to sleep."*

Slowly the excitement ebbed and I fell asleep. Four
hours later I awoke out of a deep sleep, refreshed for the
first time in almost three weeks. When my wife awoke I
told her what had happened to me during the night.
When I finished she said simply, "Well then, God healed
your attack."

She said it so—well, näively, that it annoyed me. It
seemed so simple for her to believe, but I wasn't built
that way. Six and a half years of scientific education had
taught me to be skeptical.

"My dear," I smiled condescendingly, "it is not quite
that simple. Many asthmatics have a psychosomatic problem." I hoped I was impressing her with such words as I
continued, "The spasms of the bronchial tubes, which
cause asthmatic attacks, are under the control of the sub-
conscious mind and there could well be a perfectly logical
psychological explanaton for the whole affair."

The excitement involved during the experience surely
produced a fair amount of adrenalin, which would have
had some effect on my bronchi. I was not convinced, but
I must admit the experience had made me mighty curi-
ous.

4.

The Way, the Truth and the Life

AFTER A FEW more days our rehearsals in Glyndebourne were finished and the company left for the Edinburgh Festival in Scotland. On the way up on the train, I noticed my *Boris Godunov* score in my briefcase, which I had not looked at in five months. It had remained in the case in Europe, in Argentina and back again untouched. I knew enough practical psychology to realize that I kept forgetting to study Boris because I was afraid of it. I was beaten before I began.

I spent a miserable night, which ended with a bad dream that crystallized all my fears: I was on the Met stage about to do the second-act monologue. As I began to sing, the audience began to get up and walk out. By the time I was half-finished the house was empty. I kept on singing, and one by one the members of the orchestra stopped playing, put away their instruments and began leaving. Soon they had all left—conductor, cast and stage crew as well. As the lights began going off, I turned and left the stage.

What a relief when I awakened—it was only a dream! But the dream revealed the burden and fears I carried around in my heart: I had to be successful in *Boris,* or I would never live it down with Rudolf Bing; failure might well mean the end of my dreams of being a leading singer.

Next day I was haunted by thoughts of doubt and failure, and I could feel the beginning of a severe cold. (Chalk up another mark for the psychosomatic singer—just one more reason to doubt the validity of my experience with the asthma attack!)

I continued to brood until one day Lucia and I were walking down the main street of Edinburgh.

"My girl," I said, grabbing her enthusiastically, "I've got it.'

"What's wrong, you crackling up?" asked my wife. "Jerry, people look on the street at us. Now let go of me or people think I've got it too."

"No, no! I've just thought of a gimmick that will make me the most famous Boris in America overnight."

"How you going to do that?" she inquired skeptically.

"Simple. Remember how Boris dies in the Met production? How he falls from the throne down a steep flight of six stairs?"

"Do I remember?" she sighed. "I am afraid you going to keel yourself."

"That's it," I cried.

"Now I know you got it for sure. Real crazy."

"No, no, now listen. Here's the gimmick. When I fall

down the stairs suppose I can't get up off the floor, maybe I have a fractured spine."

With grave concern she said, "That ees what I said. I am worry for you."

"Cia, I am not going to be really hurt. I am going to pretend."

Her big eyes widened incredulously, but before she could protest I pushed on.

"Try to imagine the situation: I am singing the greatest of all bass roles for the first time in my life, on the stage of the Metropolitan Opera House. I sing my last gasping words and then—the terrifying fall. The curtain closes. The audience cheers . . . but no curtain calls. Backstage there is pandemonium—Hines is injured. An ambulance is called (newspapers too), and the stricken singer is rushed to the hospital where New York's finest doctors consult X rays to see if his spine has been fractured. By the time the injury is diagnosed as a severely strained back, the story is on the front page of every paper in America. Cia, can't you see the headlines: 'Singer injured in fall at Metropolitan.' It's worth a million dollars in publicity."

"You aren't serious?" Lucia muttered.

"My dear, I was never more serious. It's nothing but an old-fashioned publicity stunt. I didn't come from Hollywood for nothing. Besides, it's foolproof. I've had a scientific education—I'll get some medical textbooks and cook up some controversial symptoms that will give the medics a hard time. It'll work."

"All right, it would work, but for gooden's sake don't ever tell anybodies about eet—eet would ruin you."

"Nobody will know except—well, I'll have to tell my mother so she won't die of concern and I'll have to tell Jim Sardos so he won't have a heart attack right in the theater."

I finished my performance in Edinburgh, and we spent several weeks vacationing and visiting Lucia's family in Italy again. When it was time to return to the States my wife said, "Darleeng, when we go to America you weel go away for concerts one month and I weel stay all myself alone in de hotel. Weeth de baby coming I am afraid all alone. Please, let me stay here weetha my father. When you come to New York I then fly to you. Please?"

I thought a bit and said, "Cia, one month from now will be just the time when you should be very careful."

Her face turned stubborn, and I compromised: "It's all right with me if you promise not to fly within a week of that danger period. All right?"

We canceled Lucia's reservation and packed my bags. I bade her goodbye again and took off for London and New York. When I arrived at the New York airport the next day Jim Sardos was waiting to greet me. We went to my hotel, had supper and then went up to my room to visit. Jim insisted I hire a publicity office to help draw attention to my forthcoming Boris, so I decided to try my own publicity stunt on him. Like Lucia, he was skeptical at first, but gradually he became convinced that the plan was practical.

After Jim had left, for the first time in a month, that strange voice spoke to me.

"Is what you are planning honest?"

"There's surely nothing wrong in doing it. I'm not hurting anyone."

"Is it honest?"

"Now see here," I reasoned, "the theater is built on fantasy. Ten years from now I could confess the deed publicly and people would admire my guts for carrying out such a bold maneuver. What would you have me do?"

"Would you do what I told you?"

"You wouldn't ask me to give this up? It's too important."

"I didn't ask you to give it up. But if I asked you to give it up, would you be willing to do so?"

"No. I wouldn't. We're dealing in a serious matter—my future, my career. It's too important for me to gamble on what is just a little thought in my head. My answer would be 'No.' "

"Do you think I would help you to write your opera on the life of Christ any more?"

"Now wait," I argued, "the more famous I get in my career the more it will promote this opera."

"I don't need your help," was the sharp reply.

"Well, the answer is still 'No!' " And there I sat, defiant and self willed. Then my thoughts turned back to that night a month before when I had had my first strange experience with that inner voice and the asthma attack.

But no! That didn't prove anything! There could be

other explanations. Yet it was strange and had an effect on me.

Suppose it were possible for a man to talk with God in this fashion—how unbelievable that was! Yet the asthma attack. . . .

Then it occurred to me for the first time that the logical conclusion might be that man could not only know God but could know His will directly, too. Imagine knowing God's will and deliberately rejecting it. What a responsibility! Better to have not known His will at all than to have known and said no.

If I were to give up this stunt I would be jeopardizing the most important thing in my life—my career. God was pitting me against my first love. Which was more important—worldwide fame or Him? My career or God? I wrestled with myself for ten minutes before I made my decision.

"God, I would rather be a comprimario singing bit parts in a second-rate theater and belong to you, than to be the greatest singer in the world and have turned you down. Tell me what to do and I swear I'll do it."

This step was blind faith, and it was a gamble which, at the moment, I feared was going to cost me my career. I stood there waiting for the inner voice to tell me to give it up or to go ahead.

Instead a thought came again like a lightning bolt, *"Open that Gideon Bible on the dresser and where you open it you will read my answer to you."*

I picked up the Bible with a sense of premonition, took

a deep breath, and flung the book open. I began to read in the middle of the twenty-fourth Psalm, "Who shall ascend into the hill of the Lord? Or who shall stand in His holy place? He that hath clean hands, and a pure heart; who hath not lifted up his soul unto vanity, nor sworn deceitfully. He shall receive the blessing from the Lord, and righteousness from the God of his salvation."

The full significance of this quote did not fully penetrate my mind at that moment, but I knew that it was a direct answer to my problem and that the publicity stunt would have to go. This was too direct an answer to be a coincidence. The chance of stumbling onto such a verse accidentally would be infinitesimal.

"You *are* God," I whispered. "I have no choice at all but to obey. All right, that publicity stunt is out."

The inner voice spoke again: *"I will repay you for this."*

That surprised me. I didn't seek any reward for my act. I did it because I wanted God and now I had found Him. No reward could be as great as this. But He had promised a reward and as I look back years later I recall that Psalm 24 had also said: "He shall receive the blessing from . . . the God of his salvation."

Another point I missed at the time was the promise hidden in the word "salvation." To me the word had no special meaning, but it applied to me as part of God's promise. I had taken Jesus Christ first in my life and the consequences were beyond my temporarily limited understanding.

The next morning when I arose, you may imagine, my whole world began to change. God was in it. I could talk with Him. He could talk with me. I would never be alone again.

Then my thoughts turned again to Boris. I still did not know the opera, and if I were to be successful now I would have to work hard and perform honestly. Where to begin? I thought of all the stage directors and colleagues with whom I had discussed the mad Czar. Everyone had a different idea as to how he should be portrayed. But what did these laymen know of psychopathology? Who could best describe a pathological condition? A psychiatrist or psychologist, of course! I was to leave the next day for a concert tour of numerous U.S. cities and would be able to consult experts. If I presented each one with the libretto I might get professional diagnoses of Boris' mental disorder and, from this technical advice, I could build a logically sound characterization of Boris Godunov.

After supper I was invited to a small party upstairs in the hotel where I was staying. There I met a brilliant, well-educated young man who worked for *Look* magazine and we got into a first-class bull session that ranged from quantum mechanics to symbolic logic. We finally called it a draw about 2:00 A.M. and went our individual ways. I went back to my room feeling like an intellectual giant. I opened the door to the room where I had had my deep and moving experience the night before, and still glorying in what I considered my intellectual prowess, I suddenly felt like a fool as I felt the Lord's presence again.

"Lord, do you want to tell me something?"

"Open that Gideon Bible on the table and you will find what I have to say to you."

"Lord, if I open that Bible and there is no message waiting for me. . . . Well, last night was a beautiful thing. And if it doesn't work tonight, then the whole thing was just a vain bubble that will pop."

"Open that Bible."

Reluctantly I went to the bureau and flipped the book open with great apprehension. It opened at I Corinthians 3:18–19: ". . . If any man among you seemeth to be wise in this world, let him become a fool. . . . For the wisdom of this world is foolishness with God. . . . He taketh the wise in their own craftiness."

I was stunned. "Lord, this obviously applies to me, but I don't understand what it means. How does one become wise by becoming a fool?"

"What is truth?"

"Well, that certainly is the prize question," I replied. "Wise men from all the ages have sought the answer to that one. I knew that truth was something one could never know in its entirety. One could only approximate to the truth. I can't answer the question. So what is truth?"

"I am truth," He replied.

"What on earth do you mean by that?" I asked.

"In the past," He said, *"you have always used your intellect to define God and truth. You shall no longer do this. You will believe first what I tell you even more than your very senses. I will lead you to the right answers. You will know nothing for sure unless I have told*

you. What I have told you, you will know for sure. Then, and only then can you use your intellect and logic to explain what I have revealed to you."

I had always been led by my intellect and, in a fashion, I worshiped it. Now I was about to learn to be led of God Himself—by His revelation. I began to think of what He had disclosed to me. What did I really know? Practically nothing. I was going to have to ask a lot of questions in the future.

The following day I left on my tour. During that month of travel, I sought out psychiatrists and psychologists and accumulated a mass of material on the personality problems of Boris Godunov. The psychiatrists and psychologists disagreed among themselves as much as laymen did as to how Boris should be portrayed. After interviewing six experts I managed to coalesce the varying viewpoints into three major personality types. I became so engrossed in the results that toward the end of the tour I wrote a paper, "The Three Faces of Boris Godunov," which was accepted for publication by the leading music magazine of that time, *Musical America*.

A few days later I received a telegram from my wife telling me she was coming home on October 25th. That was the exact day that she would be in danger of losing the child—not the day after or the day before. I looked at the day's paper for the date—it bore the same date as the telegram and counting the eight-hour time differential my wife was already on the plane flying back to the States. There was nothing I could do but wait, and the longer

I waited, the greater my anxiety. What if she lost the child again? The last blow had been so hard on her I wondered if she could stand it again.

"Lord God, do something. Please help, please." Again I was directed to open the Bible. I threw it open and began to read the last part of Psalm 113. At first the words made little sense: "Who is like unto the Lord our God who dwelleth on high, Who humbleth himself to behold the things that are in heaven, and in the earth! He . . . lifteth the needy out of the dunghill; That he may set him with princes, even with the princes of his people. He maketh the barren woman to keep house, and to be a joyful mother of children. Praise ye the Lord."

I couldn't believe my eyes at first. Then I gasped, "You mean it, Lord?"

"Yes, my son, it is my promise to you. As I am God you shall have this child."

But as soon as God makes a promise the devil says it is a lie. And so within a few hours a long-distance call came through. No one seemed to be on the line; then I thought I heard the sound of sobbing.

"Lucia, is that you?" Still just the sound of someone crying.

"Cia, answer me, is it you?"

For more than a minute she could not speak. Finally Lucia was able to pour out her troubles haltingly: She had just arrived at the hotel, after passing the whole night on the plane. She was having the same symptoms she had had when she lost the first child. The doctor wanted her to go to the hospital, but she was so afraid of losing the child she refused. He had put her to bed and told her that if the symptoms didn't stop within an hour she absolutely *had* to go to the hospital. The doctor had just left.

There was no way for me to fly home until the next morning, so I did my best to comfort her and told her to call me immediately if there was any change in her condition.

Hanging up the phone, I pleaded, "God, God, do something, please. You've got to help."

"What do you want from me, another miracle? Have I not already said that you'll have this child?"

"Yes, but she's losing it. Please do something."

"I have already done my part, now you have to learn your lesson and that is the lesson of faith. Learn to believe and trust in what I have told you. I have done all I am going to do."

Little by little my spirit began to calm down and after about half an hour I rested in trusting peace. Then and only then, did the telephone ring: It was Lucia—the symptoms had stopped. The next day I flew home to her and we were joyfully reunited.

Strangely enough, as time passed, on the nights of the sixth and seventh periods Lucia again had labor pains, but she was reluctant to call the doctor. Each time the Lord succeeded in stilling my panic, her labor ceased.

5.

What You Are Not

THE NEXT TWO months went smoothly, and as Lucia passed the last period of possible miscarriage in her pregnancy she brightened perceptibly. We began to lay plans for the arrival of our first child, the one God had promised us would soon put us on the road to being a family in the full sense of the word.

I was engrossed in my eighth Metropolitan season and was due to leave on concert tour in three weeks. Then came the news that my first Boris was scheduled for the fourth day after my return. I needed coaching rehearsals badly in order to finish memorizing Boris and to get a fluent feeling of the role, but on tour there would be no way to prepare. I would be singing every second day and traveling the day between. I bought a tape recorder and recorded the Boris with my Met coach. From the tape I could at least learn the part in my hotel rooms.

When I realized I would be spending three days in Los Angeles I telephoned Val Rosing at once. He agreed to stage Boris for me and to coach me in the role—to put himself entirely at my disposal for the whole three days.

Before I left, Jim Sardos suggested I hire a publicity

office to cover the Boris debut. (Such a practice is cus-
tomary for leading singers in the opera profession, since
many an important event can go entirely unnoticed by the
public and the press for lack of proper public relations.)
I settled on a well-known agency, and Jim came up with
so many good ideas that the agency hired him to help.
The agency discovered that I was the first native-born
American to do Boris at the Met or any other major
theater, and I began to realize what an opportunity I had.

A few weeks later in Los Angeles Val Rosing and I
closeted ourselves in his apartment and worked dozens of
hours in those three days. I learned more about *Boris
Godunov* in that short time than I had learned about any
other opera in my whole life.

By now I was extremely well-prepared and anxious to
go on the stage to face this greatest of all bass roles. When
I returned to New York the Met told me I would have
only one room-rehearsal for staging with the rest of the
cast, I was not appalled—I knew the Lord was on my side
and that somehow, some way, it would come out as He
wanted it.

Then the unexpected happened. Lucia went into labor
two weeks before she was due. We made the traditional
dash through traffic. Jim joined me in a sleepless night at
the hospital and helped me keep the waiting-room floor
well-paced.

Finally the doctor announced the arrival of a big,
healthy boy. It was Valentine's Day, February 14th, 1954.
How appropriate!

It also seemed appropriate to name him David, after

the Psalmist, whose words the Lord had chosen to comfort and reassure us for the past months. My debut as Boris was swallowed up in the joy of God's gift of a healthy strong baby who would liven our home.

During the next two days friends flooded in from all directions to see the new little one and to hear my Boris performance. Even Maestro Curci flew in from Los Angeles. My joy was complete when Mr. Bing obtained permission from the Musician's Union for me to record my Boris backstage so I could take the tape to the hospital and play it for Lucia.

On the big night, I went to the theater three hours before curtain time, after a quick visit with Lucia. I was in good voice and my nerves, understandably tense, were calmed by some pretty fervent prayer.

I have always done my own makeup and making up for Boris took me two and a half hours of painstaking work. As I added the finishing touches to the putty nose and heavy beard, Jim burst into the room, followed by Maestro Curci and Margolis, who put Jim and everyone else out so I would have peace and quiet to prepare myself for the arduous ordeal.

The assistant stage manager began the countdown for curtain time. The dark mood of the opening chorus poured out of the loudspeaker in the hall. The dressers came in and began pushing me into the heavy, rich robes of the coronation scene. My heart was beating fast—too fast—it would show in my breathing and vocal support.

"Father," I whispered.

"I am here, son. Calm down."

I did—at least reasonably so—and when I set foot on-stage my preparation paid off. All the well-rehearsed action with Val Rosing came off smoothly and easily. I was in fine voice and was able to concentrate on my interpretation with that deep sense of spiritual calm that only God can provide.

As I approached the finale—the great farewell and death scene—my mind turned to my original scheme of falling down that steep stairway. "How much better it is to do things God's way," I thought. I entered the Dumas death scene as the mad Czar, clutching a capsule of stage blood in my hand. I intended to portray Boris dying of a cerebral hemorrhage instead of the traditional heart attack. This was closer to the original Pushkin play, which I had researched thoroughly. It also nearly caused a disaster.

As I enacted the attack and plunged down the stairs for the first time, I crushed the blood capsule in my hand and smeared it on my face. (On the first fall, Boris is caught by four chorus men and carried to a chair where he proceeds to sing a touching farewell to his son.) The chorus men and I, however, had never rehearsed this bit of action. As I fell down the stairs into their arms it was obvious that the four chorusters had completely under-estimated my size and weight (235 pounds)—all five of us ended up in a pile on the stage. The much embarrassed four scrambled quickly to their feet, stumbling over their long Boyar robes, and tried to get me to the chair for my farewell speech. Then they saw my head and hands covered with blood. As they lowered me into the chair they whispered, "Jerome, Jerome! Are you hurt? Can you go on?"

I had all I could do to brush them off so I could get on with the scene. Fortunately the mood was not broken and the excitement served to make me more alert for the rest of the scene. After singing the heart-stirring farewell to my son I climbed the throne, crying out to the assembled Boyars, "I am still the Czar!" As I stood swaying at the top of the stairs ready for the dangerous fall, I breathed a prayer and thought back thankfully to the tumbling classes I had taken at UCLA fifteen years before. I plunged down the stairs headfirst, hoping I had planned correctly for what I wanted to be the most horrifying plunge ever taken on the Met stage. (Some years later, *Time Magazine,* describing one of my more recent Boris performances, offered the opinion that with the dangerous fall I was doing, there would soon be one less Boris performing on the international scene.)

Lying flat on my back, looking up at the glaring stage lights, I realized the job was finished. It was all over but the curtain calls. Friends held a reception, and afterward I stole a surreptitious visit with my wife to give her all the news and to play the tape of the performance.

During the next few days I realized that the Lord had more than kept His promise that He would repay me for giving up my publicity stunt. The reviews were beyond my greatest expectations.

"Hines Makes History at Met," one New York paper

proclaimed. "The crowd shouted itself hoarse," wrote *Time Magazine. Musical America* said it was the biggest achievement of the Met season. Mr. Bing called me in and gave me an extra performance; the next season that *Boris* was to be given I was to do the opening performance, with Dimitri Mitropoulos conducting.

My joy was completed when Lucia and I walked into our apartment the next week with our new baby. The next couple of months were naturally centered about building our home life. My mother had come from Los Angeles and was staying with us and Lucia's mother had just arrived from Italy to live with us permanently. Our apartment at Lincoln Center became a very busy place. Many times my chemistry lab a block away became a refuge, where Lucia and I could spend a few peaceful moments alone without the telephone interrupting or friends dropping in to pay their respects.

During that period of adjustment to a more complete family life a particular experience stands out in my mind. One day there was a little family problem of a rather personal nature and I behaved badly. Feeling very disturbed and no little bit guilty, I wandered gloomily over to the lab to sulk. Since we had been robbed about five times in the previous six months, I glanced irritatedly around to see if any equipment was missing. My oil immersion microscope was gone!

"How can a human being do a thing like that?" I cried.

A black opinion was forming in my mind about the anonymous character who was regularly living off me.

And I could not even take him as a dependent on my income tax. How can a human being do a thing like that?

Such a mentality was completely alien to me—and yet, was it? There had been covetousness in my heart many times. Was I not a thief in God's eyes? Anger is akin to murder, lust akin to adultery.

"Well," I concluded, looking at the empty microscope case, "people are no darn good and I'm people."

The average man regards the murderer, thief or adulterer as different as he would a Martian. Yet all of these elements slumber in the heart of every man. My mind turned back to the small but unpleasant incident in my apartment minutes before, and I sought the Lord in my heart to confess my wrong.

After being assured of His forgiveness, I said, "Lord, change me. I don't want to go on stumbling in the same way."

"Don't worry, my son, I am going to make you into what you are not."

I knew I had done wrong but I didn't think I was so hopelessly messed up as this statement indicated.

"Am I as bad as all that?" I asked, "that you have to make me into what I am not?"

"Yes, you are."

The answer with its accompanying conviction shocked and hurt me. Apparently there was nothing worth salvaging in the old Jerry Hines. I began to realize that God doesn't make better creatures out of men, but new creatures. Judging myself by the standards of my fellow man

I hadn't fared too badly; seeing myself through God's eyes was a different story.

"I am going to make you into what you are not." Well, at least He was going to do something about it. Nonetheless I was still a bit hurt. My pride was wounded. However the years that have followed have only borne out the truth of the statement as well as the desperate necessity of it. How many times when I was stubborn and resisted change, when I refused to listen to His leading I soon felt His hand painfully upon me.

He dealt the necessary blows in love, however, and they hurt only just as much as was necessary.

Now that I am His son, I have become His responsibility and I can testify that He has taken it actively over the years.

This experience left me with a very low opinion of myself and the beginning of a healthy respect for the "fear of the Lord." But naturally a knowledge of God's discipline without a knowledge of His love would create a most distorted picture. The Lord soon rectified that too.

A week later I sat in my dressing room at the Met gloomily looking into the mirror. It was a Saturday broadcast of *Tannhauser* and I was singing the Landgraf to a radio audience of 19 million people. And more, I was in terrible voice. My recent experience with the Lord made me wonder if this was another chastening for my mixed-up life. My picture of the Lord at this moment was tinged with lovelessness—principally because of the low opinion

I was forming of myself. I wanted to turn to the Lord in the trouble with my voice, but that seemed a selfish sort of act. Feeling sincerely abased I said, "God, how could anybody love a mess like me?"

"*I love you, son. I loved you enough to die for you. If you had been the only man in the world I still would have done it.*"

The truth of God's love burst upon me like warm sunshine. I was transported as I walked on the stage and, as I faced the audience, a strange effect of the bright lights made a crosslike design on the audience. I sang *Tannhauser* as I never had before.

Strangely enough, soon after that I received a letter from a friend saying, "I have seen you many times on stage but on the Saturday broadcast of *Tannhauser* your whole being radiated the peace and love of God. It was a memorable experience."

What a direct testimony this letter gave to the power and love of God shining upon me for that moment! I had been taught another essential lesson.

6.

The Holy Spirit

ALMOST SEVEN MONTHS had passed since I had come to know God. In that period I had found no one of a kindred spirit or with similar experiences with whom to share these exciting things. I learned of my fallen nature, and had become God's child. I found Him to be the Way; then I learned that He was the Truth. Certainly in the experience with our unborn child I came to know He was the Life. Then I had to face Him as Father and Lord, which taught me the values of discipline and true godly love. But there were more lessons to be learned before I was to have my first fellowship with other Christians who knew God in a real way.

When the 1954 season ended in New York, the company of 350 left for the national tour. Imagine what it is like to cram all those opera singers, conductors, dancers, stagehands, etc. i o one big train full of scenery and musical instruments, for a trip of almost two months. Sometimes we spent a whole week in a city such as Cleveland; at other times we spent one night only and boarded the train immediately following the performance. There was always a great festive air, as the company assembled at

Grand Central Station and bade good-bye to loved ones.

Lucia was there to see me off, crying quite beautifully as only she can do. It takes a rare woman to look lovely as she cries. My girl somehow manages to keep her charm in all situations.

As we left New York I knew well what was in store: an endless round of performances, receptions and balls. There would be the usual all-night poker games on the train, a great amount of socializing with colleagues you had started to know during the season, and more than plenty of carousing. Singers spend a great deal of time away from home and some of the more liberal-minded wives are resigned to their husbands' taking on a tour companions of the opposite sex for the duration of the trip. Some wives are a little less liberal minded and I have seen many marital disasters result over the years.

During this trip I sang at nine out of eleven parties in seven days. Toward the end of the tour I had overdone it a bit and I came down with a severe cold. The day of my last tour performance was at hand, and because of a windpipe infection I was dangerously close to not singing. I turned to the Lord and, for the first time in nine months, He was not there. I grew frantic realizing that in the continuous round of my social life I had completely forgotten the Lord for weeks on end. After all that had happened, how could I blithely forget Him?

I sought His Presence in vain, and finally I had to go onstage with a strange lonely feeling and fight my way through the performance. I flew home the next day, and that night, sleep was impossible. I began to pray and call on the Lord. For a full half-hour I struggled until that still, small voice spoke gently to me.

"Oh, Father," I prayed, "please, please, never go away again."

"I didn't go away, you did."

"Yes, I know, but please, don't let us be separated ever again. I don't want to lose you."

"Very well, my son. As I am God I swear to you I will never leave you as long as you live, whether you are good or bad."

These words were to sustain me countless times in the future when I would be in real spiritual need. I drifted off into peaceful sleep, but, sometime during the night— I would guess around 3:00 A.M.—I awoke and beheld a startling sight. There, reaching out of the darkness toward me, was a great arm. It looked as if it were made of some sort of hewn stone, like marble, and it glowed with a heavenly radiance. Even stranger than the vision was my reaction to it—I leaped out of bed and tried to grab it.

My wife sat up abruptly and asked, "What you do?"

"Oh, nothing . . . ," I stammered, "I was just turning over.

Just turning over in bed? I had almost turned the bed over. She studied me, scratching her head, but was kind enough to not offer any opinions. I settled back with my heart beating like a trip-hammer while she turned over and went back to sleep.

Thoughts raced wildly: What on earth was that? It

was only a waking hallucination . . . yet, why did I leap up from bed and try to grab it?

While part of my mind questioned the experience, another part of me was saying quietly, "The arm of the Lord! God has sealed His promise to me and, I know it. That is why I leaped to embrace the vision."

I had been reading a bit in the Book of Isaiah at that time, and I recalled that the "Arm of the Lord" was a name by which the Messiah was described. The implication of this experience was that my relationship to God was forever secured. I feel impelled to discuss this further.

I am reminded of the thief on the cross next to Jesus. When he asked the Lord to remember him when He came into His kingdom, Jesus *"could"* have said, "The remaining few hours of your life are going to be the most trying you have ever spent. The crowd will torment and revile you. Then you will see me, in whom you have placed your faith, die and become a lifeless piece of clay. Then the soldiers will come and break your legs with mallets so you will die faster in the most tormenting death known to mankind.

"If, throughout all this trial, you don't lose faith in me, then will you today be in paradise with me."

But we know that Jesus *"instead"* simply said, "Today shalt thou be with me in paradise."

This thief actually enjoyed a few hours of spiritual security and rest. Jesus, in His omniscience knew this man's faith was not going to fail. Now, if Jesus can know the course of a man's faith for a few hours He knows the course of our faith for the remainder of our lives. If we grant the one we must grant the other. Dear reader, if Jesus knows whether or not your faith will fail, if He knows if you are His . . . Why don't you ask Him? He will tell you if you are His forever. This knowledge will not save your soul, it is your faith that saves you, but this knowledge can save you much anguish and anxiety. Surely, it has had its effect on my life and many times when the world has seemed to fall in upon me and circumstance seemed to prove that God's love and mercy had abandoned me, I was able to recall that heart warming experience and hang on in faith to the Father I knew was mine.

Soon after the Met tour was finished I left for Buenos Aires, to do Boito's Mefistofele, the pinnacle in the Italian repertoire for bass.

The role of Mefistofele was an enormous challenge for a singer. Just four years before at the Met, Ezio Pinza had heard me coaching in Mefistofele.

"Don't sing that opera. Never," he said heatedly to me. "It will destroy your voice, I know, I tried it. Never sing it." It was a risky part to tackle, but I was young and most ambitious.

My fervor began to cool fast when I found that I couldn't sing the whole role through in one session without tiring and folding up. I tried all the harder, to no avail. I was increasingly concerned as departure time neared and I still couldn't sing it.

I arrived in Argentina tired and run-down after a 40-

hour trip—the plane broke down twice on the voyage—
and I was taken to the Teatro Colon immediately. The
new director of the company was a former head of Physical Education for the schools of Buenos Aires and a political appointee of Juan Peron, and he told me that the
dress rehearsal and the first two performances would be
on three consecutive nights. When I protested that it was
impossible to sing such a schedule he brushed off my pro-
tests, smiled, obviously in total ignorance of what the
situation meant, and said, "Oh, you can do it."

As the days passed I never sang any of the rehearsals
full voice because I knew I couldn't. Finally the night
before the first orchestra reading arrived. Now I *had* to
use my voice. The rehearsal was to start at 10:00 A.M.
—I never could sing in the morning! (When famous bass
Feodor Chaliapin was asked to sing a recital for the Boston
Morning Musicals at eleven in the morning it is reported
he answered, "I can't even spit at eleven in the morning.")

I went out to walk and pray, and after an hour of
wandering I found myself in a beautiful park with an
elevated view of the city.

"Lord," I said, "I'm not leaving this park until you
have given me the assurance that I can sing this opera."

Up to this time I had never needed God's help to sing;
my voice was one of my strong points. But now, I had to
call for help. I paced up and down that park for hours
until something happened—I knew I could sing it.

The next morning I came to the orchestra rehearsal

calm and assured and sang the role with no difficulty. I sang my way through the performances in the same manner and added another lesson to my experiences.

I was soon winging my way to Europe, and a new experience that was to build upon the fruits of my first year's walk with God. I had known and had fellowship with God, but had met no Christians for one whole year. Now all this was about to be changed.

7.

My First Fellowship

I WAS IN LONDON waiting to talk business with my agent there. In just three more days I could return home.

I was in a spiritual turmoil because recently I had again turned my back upon God and had stumbled badly in my Christian walk. After much soul searching and wrestling with sin in my life I returned to my Father. I suppose I had lingered a while hoping to regain some self respect before entering His presence.

"God," I muttered, hardly able to raise my eyes or thoughts to Him, "God, are you there?"

"Of course."

"Well I'm back."

"What took you so long?"

"I didn't feel worthy to come into Your presence."

"Are you worthy now?"

"No, I suppose not."

"I needed you. You should have returned to me immediately after you stumbled."

"But . . . " I started to protest.

"You cannot cleanse yourself, or forgive yourself. Only I can do that. When you have sinned, come to me

directly without hesitation, that I may wash your filthy hands myself."

"Well, I'm here now. . . . Forgive me, please."

"I do," was the gentle reply.

"Why do you put up with me?"

"Because I love you."

"Well—now that I'm back and you've forgiven me, what can I do to make up for this?"

"Nothing, absolutely nothing. I paid the price of your sin long ago on the cross. It is paid in full and there is nothing you can do to make it up. Nothing."

I was humiliated—out of self-respect and pride I *wanted* to contribute to my restitution. It was a helpless feeling to discover that I could do nothing. But I was beginning to learn of God's long-suffering patience and love for me.

Just then I happened to pass Hyde Park and saw a Salvation Army band playing. It reminded me that four years ago I had promised a Salvation Army officer I would sing in the Bowery—a promise that was still unfulfilled.

The Lord spoke to me again:

"You need a church and fellowship. Make it good here in London. Go look up the Salvation Army and offer your services in any capacity."

I went right to a telephone directory and searched until I found the heading, under which followed a great list of corps and services. As my finger passed the title "Goodwill Center," on Cirencester Street in Paddington, the worst slum area in London, the Lord said, *"There, that's the one."*

Too embarrassed to taxi to the Salvation Army, I walked five miles to Paddington.

It was almost dusk when I arrived at Cirencester Street. The neighborhood had definitely degenerated into a bad slum area; dirty, poorly clothed children ran about me in the street and made comments and jokes about my size and my clean clothes. I almost gave up my quest right there, but I spotted an address close to the one I wanted. I found a dismal brick building—"The Goodwill Center." I was so hesitant to enter that I bypassed the building twice before mustering enough courage to enter.

I knocked on the door unenthusiastically and a wizened old lady opened the door a crack and explained that both of the corps officers were out but would be back about 8 P.M.

I returned to the corps at that hour and was greeted by Captain Wrigley—a tall, gaunt, friendly woman in her forties. She explained that the major had been delayed, but would call me in the morning.

The next morning my phone rang early.

"Jerome Hines? This is Major Burton, Salvation Army," a clipped voice announced. "Can you be here by nine? You want to help out? Well, we'll find plenty for you to do."

Major Burton was a stocky, white-haired little man, but what he lacked in height, he made up for in sheer drive and energy. I had hardly arrived before he had me in his pickup truck. It was obvious no time was wasted in his busy day. Our first stop was to pick up and deliver lunches for fifty poor folks in a home for the aged. Then off to a home in the suburbs to bring back some old clothes and furniture. I recall he was rather upset by most of what we picked up—90 percent junk, which could in no way be reclaimed or used. We made various trips that day, stopping for a quick lunch at the Goodwill Center.

Back on the street, I opened the conversation, "Tell me, Major, how did you come to join the Salvation Army?"

"Well, sir, during the last war, I had a good job in the shipyards, but one day a voice seemed to say to me, 'Follow me,' and that very day I quit my job and joined the Salvation Army."

I looked at him thoughtfully. "A voice seemed to say to me. . . ." How similar to my own experiences! Was it possible others could share this same peculiar feeling that they could know God? I didn't express my thoughts on the subject openly however, that was to come under quite different circumstances about ten days hence.

We arrived back at the corps and spent half an hour unloading heavy ware from the truck. It was now about five and Captain Wrigley wanted to know if I'd join them at supper. I accepted happily, but warned that I had to leave immediately after for an appointment.

"Do you have friends in London?"

"No," I replied, "I have some business to conduct down at Covent Garden Opera House."

Her face became wreathed in smiles when she found out I was an opera singer, and that I sang the bass repertoire.

After supper I went home, dressed and went to the Covent Garden Opera House. But amidst the glamor and glitter of London's opera society, my thoughts remained in the slums of Paddington.

The next morning bright and early I was back at the corps. Captain Wrigley met me at the door and ushered me into the living room where we talked a bit, waiting for the Major to arrive from his home.

"And did you go to Covent Garden last night?" asked Captain Wrigley, her face lighting up in a manner I had not seen before.

"Yes, I did."

"It must have been a beautiful affair," she said. "Were the ladies all dressed up in beautiful long dresses and the men in formal attire? Do tell me about it."

As I related about the evening her eyes grew larger and larger and this plain middle-aged Captain in her simple blue uniform looked more and more like Cinderella asking about the royal ball. For a short while I had a privileged glimpse into a heart of childlike wonder, a heart that had never known a life other than dedicated service, severe self denial and spinsterhood. (Several years later I was happy to hear Major Wrigley had finally married another officer in the Army.) In those few moments she was picturing herself in a long sweeping evening gown, going to the opera. It was touching.

Just then the Major arrived and Captain Wrigley hurried back to preparing lunch. Soon the Major and I were on our way about London in the truck again.

"Have you ever been to International Headquarters?" he asked.

"No, where is it?"

"Right here in London. I thought we'd stop off there for a visit. The officers would like to meet you." Soon we parked before a large building and went in. In a few minutes, after much hand-shaking, we were sitting in the office of a Colonel on the staff. He took us on a tour of the building, of which he was obviously proud.

So were Major Burton and I.

"That's some place," said the Major, as we went back to the pickup truck. "Along that line, how'd you like to hear Hugh Redwood speak tomorrow?"

"Who's he?" I asked.

"A famous newspaper writer who went into the slums of London some years ago to write a feature story and ended up writing a book called 'God in the Slums' and got converted in the process. Now he's religious editor for one of our biggest newspapers, who spends all of his spare time traveling about the British Isles preaching about Jesus Christ. He's a great man and I chauffeur him on all his trips.

"Would you sing for us tomorrow? We're having two meetings at a men's hostel and Hugh Redwood will be speaking at the second meeting."

"Well," I said, reluctantly, "I don't mind singing, but I'd like to help out in some other way too."

"Oh, if you want to wash dishes, as you said, we'll find some dishes for you to wash too. Will you sing?"

"OK."

"By the way, look over there." He pointed to a new building. "During the war a big apartment house stood there; it was hit by a buzz bomb—a terrible disaster, so many people killed, so many trapped and wounded.

"Captain Wrigley and I had our canteen truck down here fifteen minutes after it happened. It was a desperate and dangerous job rescuing those still alive in the ruins. What a terrible sight it was. You'll never know how many headless bodies and maimed people Captain Wrigley pulled out personally. Later she received a medal from the Queen for her extreme bravery."

I looked at him incredulously, remembering the child-like, Cinderella look I had seen on her face only that morning. It was hard to connect the two personalities.

We returned to the corps to be greeted by Captain Wrigley. I treated the Captain with a new respect. After supper I got a picture of what a work of dedication the Salvation Army really is: These officers received a stipend equivalent to $15 a week, out of which they had to buy their own uniforms, food and daily necessities of life; their lodging was furnished by the Army. The picture began to emerge—austere, but beautifully and uniquely dedicated with all importance in life truly placed on a spiritual level. I was beginning to find a new breed of people I didn't know existed, those to whom Jesus Christ was their all in this world and the next. It was the beginning of a whole new and wonderful life for me as I began to find new friends living a vital Christian life.

The next morning I reported to the men's hostel where I was put right to work washing dishes. I suppose washing dishes is not such a drudgery when you don't have to do it every day. For me it was sheer pleasure to be able to serve in any way. I was to discover, little by little, the wonderful truth: the real joy in life is to serve God in any capacity that He requires. Of course the purging humility of washing dishes can be a selfish thing, or a salve to a guilty conscience, but Christian service is not meant to be that at all. It is meant to be a total response to God's will on any and all levels.

When the morning meeting was readied I was called in for prayers and to sing. I only knew two hymns, "Holy, Holy, Holy" and "Onward Christian Soldiers." It was determined that I should sing the former. I sat in the back row, anxiously awaiting my turn. At last I was going to truly sing for God for the first time in my life. The congregation sang a few hymns and then it was announced that we would have a solo. I started to get up from my chair, but the officer in charge introduced a lady-officer from another corps who arose and began to sing.

"Why," I thought, "do they let her sing? What a terrible sound. It's strange that they'd let *her* sing, knowing there's a Metropolitan Opera singer on the program."

Then my attention was caught by the radiant, beautiful look on her face and the impact of the words she was singing struck me. She sang with such dedication and sincerity that I began to forget the unpleasant scratch of her voice.

"Lord," I whispered, "it may sound bad to me, but I'll bet that is beautiful music to your ears."

Her face was aglow with a beautiful spiritual light and I was soon completely taken by her rendition. It was not art—hardly even music—but it was an experience I shall long cherish.

Then it was my turn. With no small amount of pride I flexed my vocal muscles, relishing the thought of the reaction of these simple unsophisticated officers upon hearing a leading singer from the Met.

The officer accompanying me on the piano banged out a noisy introduction in the key of C and I began to sing. To my complete consternation my voice was so scratchy and hoarse that the first line was a disaster. It got progressively worse, and I had to stop in the middle of the hymn, make a confused apology for an unexpected laryngitis attack and retreat to my seat in confusion. I don't know why, but most Christians seem to think that when they are serving God nothing—but nothing—can go wrong. It's a rude awakening when it does and I was quite shaken up. After I sat down and tried to calm my racing thoughts and embarrassment I whispered to the Lord,

"Father, what is wrong? For the first time in my life I was singing for You and You wouldn't let me. Why?" A dark thought crossed my mind and my spirit began to wilt. "Is it that I'm not worthy to sing for You?" Suddenly a clear answer came back.

"Son, you are very concerned about singing the part of Jesus Christ in our opera, 'I Am the Way.' Now, I am going to give you an apprenticeship for singing the role of Jesus. You are going to go to places I would go to—

*slums, skid rows and the like. And there you will learn to
sing for me. That woman who sang just before you sang
with true conviction, with a message that was clear and
strong. I am going to teach you to sing with a message."*

Then came the all important summation: *"I am not
interested in your beautiful voice, but in your message."*

Later that afternoon I was given another chance to
sing and this time no laryngitis prevented me. Then the
officer in charge got up to introduce the famous Hugh
Redwood.

Up stood a man who certainly did not look like a great
spiritual leader. He was fat, had stringy white hair that
hung too long in the back, and a bulbous red nose that
made him look like the old-time movie actor—W. C.
Fields. I half expected this ponderous and wheezing old
fellow to start off with, "Aha, my little chickadee."

My disillusionment was short-lived. His opening state-
me~i caused a little gasp of surprise in the hall.

"My dear friends of the Salvation Army, I have come
here with a burden on my heart to admonish you that
the Salvation Army, of all people, is almost totally neglect-
ing some very important aspects of the power of prayer.
You are not availing yourselves of all that God has in
store for you."

I was perhaps even more surprised than the rest of the
congregation. I felt that these simple folks were the most
faithful and dedicated people I had ever met—to hear this
man reproving them in such a manner was a shock.

Redwood went on to tell us the moving story of a former

newspaper colleague who was dying of cancer. The man's wife asked Redwood to visit him in the hospital, and the two journeyed there together. The colleague asked Redwood if he believed God could cure him, and received an affirmative answer, although Redwood admitted he was panicky until he heard God's voice telling him: *"Just convince him that I am here with you in this room and that I can and will heal him."*

The three in the hospital room bowed their heads in prayer for an hour, and they experienced a transformation of faith.

"This experience took place over two years ago," Redwood continued. "Now I want to read you a letter I received in the mail just two weeks ago:

> Dear Hugh, I know you'll be happy to hear that my first book has just been accepted by the publisher and at last a life-long dream of mine will be accomplished. How impossible all this would have seemed two years ago as you sat at my bedside in the cancer clinic. But now by the grace of God I have been spared to have a full and fruitful life."

Hugh Redwood concluded by citing another similar case and exhorting the assembled officers to devote more time to prayer and to seeking deeper blessing in His service. I began to realize that in only three days I had plunged into a strata of Christian fellowship I had never realized existed before. Major Burton asked me if I'd like to sing just once more that evening. His son, an officer in the Army and a band leader, was doing a program at a British Army barracks in the suburbs. I happily agreed and with that evening's concert and service the first chapter of Christian fellowship in my life came to a warm, pleasant close.

Not long after that, I left London to return to the States—to Portland, Oregon, where I was to do two performances of *Don Giovanni*. During the long hours of flying I reflected on the experiences of the previous three days and began pondering my new apprenticeship in skid-row work as preparation for singing the part of Jesus. I began looking over the music, in my brief case, which I was writing. Then, opening my Bible, I began to look for more scenes to put to music. I realized that there was so much subject matter I wanted to cover that I could never include it in one opera. I reluctantly decided I would have to broaden the scope of the work and make it a trilogy. I say reluctantly because this would take an enormous amount of time for me to compose. Then a compromise occurred to me. As soon as I finished enough scenes out of the three operas to fill one evening's time I would produce it. I would make every scene an independent vignette out of the Bible so that the work could be done in any number of ways. Then and there I decided to call the three operas, *I Am the Way, I Am the Truth* and *I Am the Life,* and the trilogy would be called, *I Am the Way, the Truth, and the Life,* from the Scripture verse John 14:6.

8.

Who Is Jesus?

DURING MY WEEK'S stay in Portland I used all my spare time reading in the New Testament and preparing the librettos for the three operas. And what I read began to disturb me. I was finding Scriptures I had never seen before. My concept of the gentle, forgiving Jesus was shaken when I read His terrible words to those who tempted Him at Jerusalem.

"Woe unto you, scribes and Pharisees, hypocrites! for ye compass sea and land to make one proselyte, and when he is made, ye make him twofold, more the child of hell than yourselves. . . . Ye serpents, ye generation of vipers, how can ye escape the damnation of hell?" (Matthew 23:15, 33).

These words made me decidedly uneasy, I was not a righteous man. And indeed, the closer I walked to God, the worse I seemed to be for I was now judging myself by His standards and not man's.

And yet, I knew God and He accepted me and loved me. But Jesus could not abide those Pharisees and consigned them to terrible judgment and they were surely ever more righteous men than I. This Scriptural image of

Jesus did not much resemble the kind, loving God I knew in my heart and a schism began to form in my thinking between the Jesus of my experience and the Jesus in the Bible. If this historical Jesus was not truly God, I was wasting my time writing an opera on his life.

Torn by this dilemma I finally took it to the Lord.

"Father," I asked, "I must have the answer to this problem. Who was Jesus? I'm confused."

"If I tell you He's a fake, will you take a public stand on it?"

That hurt—I was a conservative individual and the thought of what a public stand would mean to my family and friends was not pleasant. But I was trapped and had to continue.

"Very well, Lord, if You tell me Jesus is a fake, I'll take a public and open stand on it. Now, who is Jesus?"

"Who do you think you've been speaking to all this time?"

A wave of relief washed over me.

"But Lord, if You are Jesus—that Jesus who spoke so fearsomely to the Pharisees, how can you love a sinner like me? Is there a rational explanation for this?"

"There is."

"Will you give it to me?"

"I will shortly but not now."

My curiosity deepened as I pondered these words. My answer was due to come just a few days hence, after leaving Oregon and flying to Michigan for a concert.

I awoke late Sunday morning in the Book Cadillac

Hotel in Detroit. Just outside my window—a block from the hotel—was the edge of Detroit's skid row. I thought back to the men's hostel in London where the Lord had told me He was going to put me into skid-row work as an apprenticeship for singing the role of Jesus in my opera, *I Am the Way.*

"Lord," I said, "shall I begin my apprenticeship today?"

"Yes," was the quick reply.

I dressed and hurried downstairs for a quick brunch, and headed out through the honky-tonk fringes, into the heart of skid row. Within three minutes I was picking my way through another world! Bleary-eyed, filthy men, clothes in tatters, many with front teeth knocked out and noses flattened or broken, milled and staggered about me. Once or twice I had to step over or around a prone figure. My freshly-shaven face and new clothes made me feel like a freak, and the sea of animal-like faces seemed to regard me as such. When one of them stopped me to ask for a cigarette, the stench of stale liquor was over-whelming. After breasting this tide of broken humanity for another block, I could stand it no longer and in dis-gust—mostly at myself and my chicken-hearted attitude—started up a side street that led to a better part of town.

"Will I fail Him again by disobeying? But I can't go back and face those men."

Just then, right before me, a drunken derelict tried to do a little good. He was so soused he could hardly stand, let alone walk, but he was leading a blind man across the street. What a pitiful sight: the old man with his white cane, his poor, drunken helper wobbling alongside, trying to get him safely across the street. Tears burned my eyes and I whispered, "God, if he, in his condition, can do that to serve You, I can at least go back to skid row."

I retraced my steps with new determination and continued my search for a place to serve. Within a block I saw a Salvation Army sign. My heart leaped—I could tell them of my experience with the Army at International Headquarters in London, and I would not feel so out of place and awkward.

"Here it is, Lord, shall I go in?"

"No, Son, I don't need you here today."

My heart sank; I realized I would again have to walk in as a stranger to some mission and ask to help out. Embarrassment welled up within me.

"Please, Lord . . . ?"

"No. Keep walking."

I continued on my way and soon I had passed the Salvation Army Harbor Light and seemed to be almost at the end of the slum area.

"Lord, I'm about to leave skid row. Shouldn't I go back?"

"Keep walking, son."

After another half-block I spied a sign that said "Detroit City Rescue Mission."

"Is this it, Lord?"

"Yes, son, go in."

I strode toward the dingy building. About 150 men

stood in a soup line waiting to be fed. I was too shy to push my way through the wretched-looking crowd to enter the mission. I walked past the front door and down to the corner. Stalling for time I began to slowly walk around the block.

"Are you going in or not?"

It was Paddington all over again.

"I'm going. Just give me time to brace myself."

Then I saw an alley going behind the mission.

"Lord, may I go in the back way?"

"Certainly."

I headed down the alley, and there behind a cyclone fence, was a mission pickup truck. A man was sitting in the truck reading a newspaper.

I called over to him, "Who's in charge here?"

"You wanna see Reverend Brooke?" he asked.

"I suppose so."

"Come on."

The man descended from the truck and led me in the back door. We wended our way up the stairs into the minister's office.

"My name is Jerry Hines and I'm here in town for the day with nothing to do." I shifted my feet uncomfortably as I continued, "I wonder if I might help out in some way in the mission—like washing dishes or—any sort of work will do."

His answer was simply, "No!" He just stared at me, and my discomfort increased.

"Do you have a service tonight?" I stammered, "You see—I'm a Metropolitan Opera singer and maybe—well, could I sing on the service?"

"No!" The cold reply left me speechless. Then he added, softening a bit, "An outside church is giving the service tonight, and I don't think it's wise to interfere with it."

He continued to stare at me but said nothing—not even "Get lost."

I took a deep breath, sighed "Thanks a lot," and headed for the door.

"Just a moment, young man," he called. "Is there anything I can do for you?"

"No," I said flatly, feeling a little twinge of satisfaction at giving him his own treatment.

"Have you been saved?" he queried.

I associated such a question with some kind of sawdust-trail, cornball religion so I rejoined skeptically, "You tell me what you mean by that, and I'll tell you if I have been."

Pointing his finger at me he said, "Do you think you can please God with good works?"

"Shouldn't He be pleased?"

"What I mean is, do you think you can work your way into heaven by doing good works?"

"I don't know," I shrugged, "I never thought about it."

"You never thought about it?" he asked. "Then what are you doing here? Why did you ask to help out in

At twelve

Below: The Lincoln Center lab

Opera News, December 7, 1953

Rehearsing Boris with Val Rosing. *Below:* Chatting with Gennaro Curci

Photography by Lyn Riker

Christmas, 1965. *Below:* Steady, boys!

Photography by Wallace Litwin, Pix, Inc.

Photography by Payne, N.Y. Daily News

Christmas, 1959

Photography by O. Henry Hertzler, Lancaster New Era, Lancaster, Pa.

Witnessing

Photography by Lyn Riker

Photography by Karl A. Parshall, J

Rehearsal

I AM THE WAY

Performance

As Mefistofele *(Faust)* in Leningrad

Boris Godounov

the mission if you're not trying to buy God's affection with good deeds? What, then, are you doing here?"

I was faced with a dilemma. I knew why I had come, but I had never let my hair down and told anyone but my wife about my conversations with the Lord.

"Well?" he demanded

"Look, I came here because the Lord sent me."

"You'd better tell me what you mean by that."

"Very well." I sat down in front of his desk and began to relate the whole story of my experiences with the Lord. As I spoke, his interest grew. I told of my experience in Portland and how the Lord had promised to show me how He could love me and be so against the Pharisees, and how I had come to the mission.

"Why," he exclaimed, "you're saved and don't know it. I never thought such a thing was possible. Look here," he took out a Bible. "Here is the explanation of what you're looking for." Hastily he flipped the pages to Ephesians 2:8,9.

"For by grace are ye saved through faith; and that not of yourselves: it is the gift of God: Not of works, lest any man should boast."

He continued, "You're saved because you're trusting Christ on the cross, that He died to redeem you from your sins. It is not good works that buy a man's way into heaven. It is his faith—then his good works come as result of his salvation. You're not here trying to reach heaven, you're here because God sent you. You already trusted in Him and belonged to Him, and you are here as a son obeying his Father.

"Look, maybe you *can* sing on the service tonight. I'll call the minister who is doing the program."

He dialed a number, and after a brief conversation asked me, "Do you have someone to play the piano for you?"

"I'm sorry, but my pianist is not scheduled to arrive in Detroit until 10:30 tonight." (Emil Dannenberg was my accompanist for this part of the tour; he and I had performed together since we were in college together in 1939.)

"All right," said the Reverend Brooke, hanging up the phone. "The minister's wife will play for you. Now what are you going to sing?"

"Well," I answered hesitantly, "I only know two hymns —"Holy, Holy, Holy" and "Onward Christian Soldiers."

"You can't sing those here," was the sharp reply.

A bit ruffled, I said, "What's the matter, aren't they Christian hymns?" I had just sung them for the Salvation Army in London—they weren't good enough for this mission?

"Oh, they're Christian hymns all right," he smiled. "The trouble is, you're not singing to Christians tonight. Actually their very lives are a testimony to the fact that they're not Christians. Mr. Hines, we're not interested in your beautiful voice. We're interested in your message."

My heart jumped at these words—words identical with those the Lord had spoken to my heart almost two weeks before, when He had commissioned me to go into skid-row work.

The pastor continued, "You have to bring a message in your song that is so strong that it will lift a drunken derelict in the third row to his feet and bring him to the altar for Christ." He got up and returned with a hymn book in his hand. He thumbed through it and finally said, "Here, sing something like this." He handed the open book to me and I read:

> Blessed Assurance, Jesus is mine!
> Oh, what a foretaste of glory divine!
> Heir of salvation, purchase of God. . . .
> This is my story, this is my song:
> Praising my Saviour all the day long.

Thus I began to sing music with a message. At the hotel I was dressing for the meeting when the phone rang. I picked it up and heard the rough voice of Emil Dannenberg, my accompanist.

"Emil, where are you calling from? Ohio?" I asked.

"Naw, I'm down in the lobby."

"Come on up," I said.

I wondered what he was doing here so early. He was supposed to have gone directly to his cousin's house to spend the night. I asked him how come he was here.

"I just changed my reservation on an impulse," he said, when he reached my room. "And I came directly to the hotel from the airport just in case you'd like to rehearse."

"All right," I answered, "We have a concert tonight." I finished adjusting my tie. "Let's go."

He walked by my side in total silence all the way through skid row without so much as a questioning glance. At last we arrived at the mission, and I announced to Emil, "This is it."

Pastor Brooke had informed me that he could not be present at the service, so I sought out the new minister.

"You must be Mr. Hines. Thank God you came. None of my people showed up, and I'm alone on the platform." His face fell, "But my wife was taken ill suddenly and was not able to come. I have no one to play the piano for you."

"Don't worry," I said. "The Lord has provided for that too. Here is my pianist, Mr. Dannenberg. He can play for me."

"Can he play our hymns too?"

"Yeah," said Emil cryptically.

The minister sighed with relief, hurried us to the platform, and the meeting began. During the course of the service several of the men in the congregation came forward crying and broken to accept Christ. I stared at them in wonderment. Did my little part in the service have anything to do with their surrender? Did I have the ability to move men's hearts with my voice? Could God really use me in this way? Did coming to the altar in such drunken stupors really mean that a permanent change, a real change, was to come about in their hopeless lives? How hopeless they really were, I was soon to learn, and how their lives could be transformed as well.

After the meeting we bid the minister good-bye, I put Emil in a taxicab and wandered the streets for two hours, going over the day's events in my mind.

How miraculously God had directed my life this day. There was no question that I had been where He wanted me. He had so met every need.

How thankful I was that I had heeded His leading and passed the Salvation Army by to take the harder road. I was beginning to learn to be sensitive to the leading of the Holy Spirit and the necessity of obedience, in order to find His fullest blessings.

9.

Circle of Protection

THERE IS NOT enough space in one, or even two or three books to tell of the many wonderful examples of God's guidance in my life. Here are a few happenings, which proved to have greater significance than appeared obvious when they occurred.

My work in the skid rows of America grew steadily. Although I avoided any fanfare about my work in America's spiritual garbage heap, word got around soon enough. Every time I got in touch with a Salvation Army Harbor Light in skid row I would receive a couple of calls from local headquarters to come and sing for some annual meeting or to preach to their advisory board. Not that there was anything wrong with that, but I was called to serve the down-and-outer on a particular mission. Soon the churches got wind of it, and before I left on any tour, dozens of requests poured in asking me to fellowship and sing at the local church during my stay in town. Christians who are concerned about keeping the Sabbath a day of rest should think twice about asking me to sing at a Sunday morning service, after a full concert the night before!

I, who had not yet learned to say "No," felt obliged to fill each request as though the Lord had sent every one for me to accept. That this was not the case was quite obvious after a year or two had passed and my seemingly inexhaustible voice began to sag under the load of singing and speaking.

One day the Reverend Wimbish, of Calvary Baptist Church in New York, called and said, "I was talking with Billy Graham the other day; he has heard of your work in the slums, and I suggested that he put you on his team for his New York crusade next spring. So you will probably hear from someone soon."

Within a day or two the call came and I accepted the chairmanship of the music committee. I was honored to be chosen, for I had a great respect for Billy Graham. It proved to be a wonderful experience, and it also led to an invitation to sing at the Presidential Prayer Breakfast in Washington, for President Eisenhower. When I arrived to sing I discovered that I had not been asked to give my testimony. I felt that this was the most important part. What God had done was what counted, not what I could do. So just before I sang, I told the President and the assembly that I had a policy that I didn't sing for nothing unless I was allowed to give my testimony. I gave it, and I have used that trick ever since.

After the breakfast I met Bill Jones, the Christian businessman from my home town of Los Angeles, who hosted and paid for the Presidential Prayer Breakfast every year.

We hit it off together immediately and a warm friendship began that was soon to grow into exciting Christian service together in the future.

The next year's Prayer Breakfast was to follow immediately after President Kennedy's inauguration. Again I was asked to sing. It was an exciting situation: I would be the first person to give a testimony to America's first Catholic President. I paced the streets of Washington for an hour before the breakfast seeking the mind of the Lord. I made up all sorts of silly gimmicks such as, "Mr. President, several years ago I discovered a 'New Frontier' in Jesus Christ." Finally, I discarded them all and begged the Lord for an answer.

"Son," He said, *"you have nothing to say to the President today. I am just as interested in reaching some bus boy waiting on one of the tables, so don't try to make some earth-shaking statements to President Kennedy. Just tell everyone there what I have meant to you."*

It changed the whole aspect of the situation. I relaxed and the testimony and song came off without a hitch. It must have made an impression, because I was invited to sing two weeks later at the annual White House Correspondents' Dinner for Kennedy. Six months later the President asked me to sing at the first State Department dinner at the White House. I also had the opportunity to sing a fourth time for him at his last Prayer Breakfast, just half a year before his assassination.

As I reflected on the number of times I was singing in Washington I realized that just a few short years ago, when we had our first son, the Lord had promised me through the 113th Psalm: ". . . [He] lifteth the needy out of the dunghill; That he may set him with princes, even with the princes of his people."

Strange how the thread of these experiences began in the dunghills of America—the skid rows—and ended up in Washington, singing and telling of Christ to two presidents of this country.

Not long after this I went on a concert tour and was all alone one evening in Cleveland. I felt restless and vaguely out of sorts until I realized that I was out of fellowship with the Lord. I left my room and walked the dark streets, determined not to stop walking until I was right with the Lord. I kept walking and praying, "Lord, I want to be where you want me to be, doing what you want me to do."

I heard someone say, "Hey, you're Jerome Hines."

The last thing I wanted to do was stop and make small talk with a perfect stranger, who had probably seen me on TV. I wanted to talk with the Lord, not this fellow who approached me.

"I went to the same high school you did—Fairfax."

Wasn't that great! I determined to shake him as fast as I could and get back to spiritual matters, but he made small talk, walking alongside me for about a block. Then he said, pointing across the street, "There's my hotel. How about a cup of coffee?"

"Sorry, I have something I have to do. It's very nice

meeting you." I shook his hand and left him standing on
the corner as I crossed the other way with the green
light. As I got across I said, "Now, Lord, where do you
want me to be, and what do you want me to do for
you . . . ?"

Then a feeling struck me. I had just missed the boat.
I turned and watched the man I had just left cross the
street dejectedly and enter his hotel. I had the crushing
conviction I should have gone with him. I continued to
try to pray, but my thoughts were disturbed and I got no-
where. Ten minutes later I walked back in the opposite
direction and just as I started to pass the hotel the same
fellow walked out the door again. He looked up: "Oh, it's
you again. How about that cup of coffee?"

"I think so," I said, chuckling at another of the Lord's
coincidences. It turned out that he was a Christian too,
as down in the dumps spiritually as I and needed Christian fellowship badly. We had a wonderful time of blessing together, and after some prayer together, we swapped
addresses and parted, both rejoicing in God's goodness in
supplying our need.

A peculiar follow-up to this story is that six months
later I arrived in Washington to judge a vocal competi-
tion. Again I felt restless and out of sorts with the Lord.
I went out to walk and, impressed by the similarity of the
situation, I said, "Lord, can't you do something for me
just as you did in Cleveland? Won't you send someone to
me here in the street as I'm walking?"

Within two minutes I was startled by a voice saying,
"Praise the Lord. You're Jerome Hines."

I turned to look at a young man.

"By the way you said that you must be a Christian," I observed.

"You bet I am," he said. We walked along about six blocks, making small talk, but in view of the circumstances I felt there must be something important for us to discuss. I was disappointed when he said, "Well, I have to turn off here now, it's been nice talking to you."

"Maybe the situation was not as significant as I thought," I mused. I wandered on, bought a hamburger and a malt and then proceeded to get thoroughly lost in the maze of streets. I was just about to stop and ask directions to the club where I was staying, when I heard a familiar voice say, "Oh, no, not you again!" It was the same young man I had left half an hour before. I knew there was a purpose in this meeting.

"Look here, I think the Lord wants us to have a talk," I said. We sat on a park bench, and the young fellow poured out a long tale of woe. If anyone needed spiritual uplift it was he. We, too, parted in an entirely different mood after prayer and the swapping of addresses.

On the surface these two incidents don't have any particular importance, but they were to contribute to an interesting and significant chain of events in the near future.

One day early in 1961 Sol Hurok called and said, "I've arranged a tour of Russia, and you are to sing *Boris Godunov* in Moscow."

What an opportunity! Imagine singing Boris at the Bolshoi Opera! I would have to relearn it in Russian—that would be a real chore, because I'd have to get a speaking acquaintance with the language, and I had heard it was a tough one. The days of singing a foreign language by rote were long past. On the Met stage you can get away without knowing a word of the language because the New York audience generally doesn't know any more about the language than you do and couldn't care less. But, if you sing in foreign countries in the native language, you have to know and feel each word, and the acting and interpretation become of great importance.

My mind came back to Mr. Hurok. ". . . and you will leave for the Soviet Union next April. That will give you a whole year to prepare," he was saying.

"Next April?"

"Yes, April."

"But Mr. Hurok, I am contracted to the Met from the middle of April until June first. I can't go then. You'll have to postpone it."

"That's impossible. The Russians are very temperamental. If you ask them to postpone something, they just cancel. It's too risky to try. If you want to go to Russia you'll have to go in April."

"But, I have a contract."

"Look, you go to Bing and tell him to let you out of the tour. There's nothing else to do."

"What a pretty mess," I thought. "The chance of a lifetime to sing Boris at the Bolshoi in Moscow, and I can't because of a contract for the Met tour, and a contract to sing roles about which I couldn't care less."

Disconsolately I called the Met and explained my situation to Rudolf Bing. He told me that it was absolutely essential I go on the tour for which I was contracted.

For the next month I continued to argue with Mr. Bing and Mr. Hurok with no tangible results. I was becoming increasingly desperate. Then Mr. Hurok agreed to try, on his next trip to Russia, to have my trip postponed. I spent weeks of agonizing waiting, alternately hoping for the best and fearing the worst.

Then Sol Hurok telegraphed the news: I could go to Moscow in late September 1962, and then tour the Soviet Union for another four weeks!

I bought some Russian grammar books immediately and began to pore over the alphabet, vocabulary and grammar. What a language! I thought German was hard but compared to Russian it was like learning pig-latin.

I don't believe I ever worked so hard in my life as I did preparing this opera. The months passed quickly, and every morning and evening I crammed my head with Russian on the commuter train between New Jersey and New York. Not until a year had passed and I had acquired a 1500-word vocabulary in Russian did I begin to relearn the Boris.

My drama coach, Val Rosing, was beside himself with excitement over my pending trip. As a young man in Leningrad, his great ambition had been to sing at the Maryinski Theater in that city, as well as at the Bolshoi in Moscow, but the Russian revolution cut that dream short. As Trotsky's secretary, he had to flee to London to save his life. Now he felt I would fulfill his lifelong

dream for him and, since he was in New York as stage
director for the City Center Opera, he insisted on working endlessly with me.

Next came a contract from Teatro Colon in Buenos
Aires for *Don Carlos* again. I would have to fly directly
from Buenos Aires to Russia, but that would be good for
me because *Don Carlos* was always good for my voice,
and should put me in good form for my Moscow debut.
The only trouble would be the long two-day trip and the
time change of nine hours. I would have to sing within
four days of my arrival, which wasn't a great deal of time
to acclimatize myself to the Moscow weather and to the
different time.

That June a close friend, Dr. Arthur D'Alessandro, per-
suaded us to take a house at the Jersey shore near his
summer home.

A few weeks later I called my lawyer, Albert Gins, and
said I had not received my visa for Buenos Aires.

"Have you read the morning papers? Maybe you're not
going to Buenos Aires at all. It looks as though they're
going to have a revolution . . . but I'll send a telegram
reminding them about the visa, anyway.

"Then that settles eet," Lucia stated flatly, when I
told her the news. "We don' go to Buenos Aires."

"Are you kidding? We have a lot of money involved
and our economy for the summer was based on this contract. If you're worried, I'll go alone."

"Oh no," she returned, "you are a father for tree boys.
You're not a go risk your life. The boys need you."

And so the argument got hotter and hotter. Then I stopped a moment, reflected and said, "Look, it doesn't matter what you or I want. What really matters is what the Lord wants. Now sit down and pray with me for an answer—and we'd better get the same answer."

Reluctantly she sat down and we both began to pray silently. Eventually I felt I had a weak answer of "yes." But I had no feeling of real assurance about it. I opened my eyes until Lucia finished praying. When she did I said, "Well."

"My guidance tells a me to read the newspapers for next a two weeks. Then I decide."

"Some guidance," I smirked.

"Thatsa my answer."

"OK I'll go along with you. It makes good sense." So we put off the decision. Each day we read the newspapers, and each day the news got worse. I began to get some real qualms about the advisability of going, but I kept putting off making the decision, hoping things would get better. Then, one night as we were preparing to go to bed, I had a familiar sensation. I felt the Lord's presence about me, but in a way I had never experienced before. Spiritually, I felt as though I were in the middle of a hurricane. And I knew with a terrible urgency that I must go out and be alone to speak with the Lord.

I slipped into my clothes and literally ran out the front door into the starry night. By now I felt as though the Person of the Lord was roaring about me.

"What is it, Lord," I cried to the heavens. "What do you want to tell me?"

"Son, I'm going to do a most unusual thing. I'm going to put a circle of protection around you for two months so the devil cannot touch you in any way."

"Lord," I said, "you said two months. Does that mean we're going to Argentina too?"

"Absolutely. You and your wife are going, and have no fear. Satan cannot touch you. But there is more, my son. Eight years ago when you gave up your publicity stunt in Boris and I said I would repay you, you thought I did. Son, that was not payment in full. Payment in full will come in Moscow. I have prepared something for you there that will be so stupendous, so fantastic that when it happens you will not be able to believe it. Now go on your trip with my blessing and have a glorious time."

I felt as though I were walking two feet above the ground, as I tramped the seashore for over half an hour before I returned to the cottage. Waking my wife, I said, "Lucia! Pray. Pray now and get your guidance on our trip to Argentina." She bowed her head for a moment, then looked at me uncertainly.

"We're not going . . . ?" she queried, timidly.

"We *are* going. The Lord just told me," I said forcefully. Something in my face struck her dumb. I told her the whole story of what had happened and something about my manner completely convinced her.

"I know it wasn't God telling me not to go. I was afraid."

"Don't be afraid. The devil can't touch us in any fashion. God promised." She accepted this completely and did not voice a single doubt. Somehow the assurance the Lord had given me carried over to her.

The next morning we saw Dr. D'Alessandro and his wife, and I related the entire experience to them, and I am glad I did for there are now two more witnesses to this story. I then called my lawyer and told him to get busy with Argentina and get me that visa.

"I don't think there is anyone there to issue a visa now," he stated flatly. "Read the morning paper. 40,000 troops are out in the streets with tanks, and they have blown up the bridge between the two rival army factions. You surely don't intend to go now?"

"Get the visa," I said.

"All right, it's your neck."

But as soon as God makes a promise, the devil tries to make it seem a lie. The very next day my visa arrived, and I went into New York to take care of the business details. I stopped off at the Hurok office to see if there was any last minute news on Russia before I left. Walter Prude, Mr. Hurok's right-hand man, greeted me.

"Well," he said, "I hope you're not still planning to go to Argentina."

"Yes, I am. The visas just arrived and Lucia and I leave in two days."

"Isn't it pretty risky to go at a time like this?"

"Don't worry," I said firmly, "nothing will happen to us." He didn't share my confidence and I was not about to offer further explanations that would probably only serve to make him doubt my sanity.

He then pulled out a telegram and said, "Well, the information you've been waiting for is here."

Eagerly I looked over his shoulder as he read it aloud. It stated that I would work with the Novisibirsk in Moscow, then Leningrad, Kiev and Tblisi.

"What's this Novisibirsk bit?" I asked.

"I don't know," said Walter. "Let's go ask Sol." We walked into Mr. Hurok's office and after the usual congenialities, Walter asked, "Mr. Hurok, what is this about Novisibirsk?"

"Oh," said Hurok, "the Bolshoi Opera Company is not doing *Boris* this season. They have taken it out of the repertoire to mount a new production of it for next season. So you can't do it with them. But the company from Novisibirsk in Siberia is touring to Moscow at that time and is doing *Boris* at the new Kremlin Theatre. They have agreed to let you do the Boris with them."

It took a moment for the meaning of these words to sink in.

"You mean—I'm not singing Boris with the Bolshoi in Moscow at all?"

"I'm sorry Jerome; it's not even in the repertoire. But you'll be doing Boris in Moscow just the same."

"Mr. Hurok," I cried out, "you wouldn't bring a leading singer from the Bolshoi here to debut with the City Center in New York. You'd bring him to the Metropolitan. And I don't intend to go all the way to the

Soviet Union just to sing with a secondary company in Moscow. You wire right back to Moscow and get me a debut with the Bolshoi in some other opera like *Faust*, but no *Boris* with a company from Siberia. That's final."

"Jerome," said Hurok firmly, "trust my judgment. You must debut in *Boris* in Moscow. Nobody here will know the difference—the Bolshoi or the Novisibirsk. All they'll write in the New York papers will be, 'Jerome Hines sings Boris in Moscow.' Besides Novisibirsk has a very good opera company. But your debut in Moscow must be in *Boris*."

I yielded, but a burning bitterness was growing in my heart. I had studied a year and a half to sing with the Bolshoi, now I was being humiliated.

"All right, Lord," I whispered between gritted teeth, "if you don't want me to sing at the Bolshoi . . . then I don't want to sing there either." Angry tears burned my eyes during the two-hour drive back to Seaside Park at the shore. I fought to yield myself to God's will. If He had so desired this would not, could not, have happened. He sent this disaster and He had His reasons which I, at this moment, surely couldn't see, but I acknowledged His sovereignty and bowed myself before Him. But it wasn't easy. I have, over the years, not found myself to be the wonderful, easy going, victorious Christian that others seem to be. In fact the remainder of this book will prove just that. It is a testimony to God's faithfulness alone, no credit to me.

I finally reached home and gave Lucia and the

D'Alessandros the bad news. Dr. D'Alessandro suggested
that singing with the Novisibirsk instead of the Bolshoi
might be a blessing in disguise since I wouldn't be as
nervous, and could do a better job. I agreed with this
rationalization reluctantly and tried to act cheerful about
it, although I surely didn't feel it.

We took off early in the morning on the long but un-
eventful flight to Argentina. My Argentine agent was
waiting, and after we passed through customs, we got into
a cab and began the long trip into the center of town.
My wife was full of questions about the revolution. My
agent calmed her with the news that the opposing generals
had just agreed that afternoon to sit down at the conference table and work out a peaceful solution. Lucia was
almost convinced, when two soldiers with rifles sprang suddenly onto the road ahead of our taxi and forced us to
stop. Lucia made herself as small as she could in the back
seat clutching my arm with a death grip. There was a
spirited conversation between our driver and the soldiers.
As we pulled over to the curb, Lucia whispered, "What's
a happen?"

My agent chuckled and said, "Don't worry. They just
want us to push that stalled car up ahead so he can get
going." I laughed at Lucia, but I must admit I was relieved myself.

We settled down in a hotel, and after a hot bath and
an excellent meal, we spent a peaceful night except for the

occasional distant sound of a Molotov cocktail or chanting in the streets.

The next morning we walked to the theater and greeted our old friends there. All seemed much better arranged than it had been on my last visit there eight years before.

The general manager turned to the stage director and asked, "So—are we going to do the revolution or not? Is it decided?"

Lucia leaped to her feet and cried out, "Revolution? When?"

"No, no, Senora," said the general manager, placatingly, "we are speaking about the revolutionary scene in the third act of *Don Carlos*. We have discussed whether it should be cut or not."

We all had a good laugh at Lucia's expense, then I was sent upstairs for an ensemble rehearsal with the conductor, Maestro Previtale.

Work began in earnest and the next two weeks were spent between the theater, our hotel and various restaurants. I was a little worried, because after almost a month's vacation from singing my voice did not feel in the best of form. Teatro Colon was one of the most discriminating and important theaters in the world and, furthermore, I was thinking beyond to the Russian tour.

One day a two-page telegram arrived from Moscow: The leading bass of the Novisibirsk Opera had been electrocuted and killed in his bathtub; the company had

canceled their tour to Moscow, leaving me with no performance there. Mr. Hurok's representative in Moscow,
Ralph Parker, had gone to the government agency that
arranged all foreign cultural events for the Soviet Union
and protested, mentioning that just a few months before,
Roberta Peters, the leading coloratura from the Metropolitan Opera Company had received her visa so late that
she couldn't make her Moscow concert and had canceled
the entire tour. Now Jerome Hines had lost his only
Moscow appearance and would probably cancel his tour
also. This would cause an international incident—possibly jeopardize the cultural exchange. The next day the
Bolshoi Opera announced that they would do one special
performance of *Boris Godunov* for Jerome Hines.

This was too much. A man had to die for me to sing
Boris with the Bolshoi! Sobered considerably, I took my
thoughts to the Lord.

"Father, is it so important for me to sing Boris at the
Bolshoi that a man had to die?"

As Lucia and I read the remainder of the telegram,
which gave the dates for my appearances in the Soviet
Union, an incredulous look came to her face.

"Are they crazee?" she asked. "Nobody can sing a
schedule like thees—four weeks of performances crammed
into three weeks. You can't do eet, darleeng. You must
cancel something."

"Look, Cia, I'll try it as is, and if it gets too hard I'll
cancel."

She looked at me skeptically; she knew I was not the canceling type. "Well, you better be in a good condition when you get there. Thees ees important. So take good care of yourself."

The next day was the *Don Carlos* dress rehearsal. I sang pretty well, but not up to my usual standards, and the next morning Lucia was still brooding over it.

"You didn't sing your best," she accused. "What you going to do, arrive at Moscow in bad voice? You don't take care yourself as an opera singer should. You want to ruin yourself in Moscow? The whole world weel be watching you. Thees ees no leetle thing."

I was already nervous and touchy about the situation. We exchanged a few words and I said something rather unkind. She burst into tears, took her purse and slammed out of the apartment. I sat there steaming for a while and then began to feel guilty—I hadn't really needed to be so harsh. Finally I said, "Lord, I guess I was wrong this time."

"*Yes, you were,*" was the severe reply.

It is one thing to be big enough to admit you've been wrong, but did the Lord have to rub salt into the wound by agreeing with me so quickly?

"Oh, Lord," I said, "I just wish she'd come back so I could apologize." But she didn't. I sat and stewed until I was so miserable I couldn't stand it. I threw on my jacket and coat and stalked out of the hotel too. As I wandered the crowded streets aimlessly I only felt worse.

"God, my little darling is walking these streets—miserable and crying. Please—do me a favor and do what you did in Cleveland and Washington: You led me to someone then, when I asked you. Please do it again; take me to Lucia, wherever she is."

What a foolish request—in a great city of eight million inhabitants I expected the Lord to lead me right to Lucia.

"Walk in faith, my son."

"Oh, Lord, please?"

"Walk in faith and I'll do as you asked."

I began walking down Calle Florida, lined with beautiful shops.

I spotted an arcade of shops where Lucia was fond of window-shopping.

"That's where she is," I decided. "She's in that arcade buying up everything she can get her hands on, just to spite me." I walked swiftly down the long corridor between the chic shops.

"Son," the Lord broke into my thoughts, *"don't underestimate your wife. Now you go back to the street and continue to walk in faith."*

Another three minutes of walking brought me to the park in which eight years ago I had had my great spritual battle before my Mefistofele. Ever since then that park has had a warm place in my memory. Had my wife been mysteriously drawn to this spot? I had never taken her there; she didn't even know it existed.

I began to experience that peculiar spine-tingling assurance that comes when all the pieces of the picture in guidance begin to fall into place. I crossed the circular boulevard that leads to the park, climbed the steps that lead into it, and began to walk under the large, spreading trees that sheltered most of it. I spotted a diminutive figure that looked very familiar, seated fifty yards ahead, her back to me. My heart pounded with joy and thankfulness as I walked up and sat down next to Lucia. Her eyes widened in surprise; she gaped at me a moment.

"How did you find me here?"

"I asked the Lord to bring me and He did."

She burst into tears. "Oh, I was just sitting here wishing you would walk by and I would see you." She was a mile and a half from the hotel and way off the beaten path! (I take special joy in telling this incident because like many of God's miracles, one leads to another and another in a beautiful chain of events. The experiences in Cleveland and Washington had led to this event, which in turn was to lead to another of much larger consequence.)

The next day the opening of *Don Carlos* came off successfully. The next performance went well also, but the weather in Buenos Aires, which is traditionally abominable, finally caught up with me and my Met colleague Regina Resnick, who was singing Eboli. Both of us were indisposed enough for the management to postpone the following performance by two days. This gave us time to recuperate sufficiently to do a good job, but I still couldn't seem to shake the infection lodged in my windpipe.

When the last performance came to a close, Lucia and I drew a sigh of relief. The entire month we spent there, threats of revolution rumbled continually, but the generals continued to sit at the conference table and argue. It seemed we might get out before any trouble broke loose —the circle of protection was holding, as the Lord had promised.

Next morning we boarded the plane for Zurich, first stop on our way to Moscow. As we winged our way to Europe I reflected on the difficulties ahead: The schedule was nearly impossible. I had to sing only four days after my arrival—with a nine-hour time difference would I be acclimatized by then? I worried about my Russian; I had studied hard, but I had never actually sung Boris in public in that language. Then I felt the Lord's presence.

"Son, on your entire tour of the Soviet Union, I want you to fast once a week without fail."

"I can't afford to fast on this trip. I'm going to need all the strength I can muster for that murderous three weeks."

"More than physical strength, you are going to have to have a spiritual discipline such as you have never known in your life. To face this ordeal you must fast once a week."

Concerned and taken aback, I agreed reluctantly.

10.

Boris in Moscow

LUCIA and I looked out of the Paris airport window at the large, trim, powerful-looking Russian jet that was to carry us to Moscow. The word *Aeroflot* (the name of the Soviet government's international airline) was inscribed in Cyrillic symbols on the plane, as were the letters "CCCP," which stand for the Soviet Union of Socialistic Republics.

After a long wait the flight was called, and we went to the boarding gate, where we were informed that all cameras must be packed in our luggage or turned over to the hostess temporarily. We were seated right over the powerful jet engines that were at the base of the wing and were actually part of the fuselage. This contributed much to the noise and vibration of the plane, but in no way detracted from its power or efficiency—it was the first of many lessons that showed that although many of the Russian products were not as sophisticated as ours, they lacked nothing in efficiency. (We soon learned that the Russians can be very practical. For example, at the Moscow airport, which has problems with snow and ice, the airplanes are warmed up for service by a simple, but effective, expedient: A truck, with a big jet engine mounted on it, is backed up to the airplane and the hot blast of the jet's engine is turned directly on the plane's engines and fuselage. The same jets are tilted downward at a sharp angle and used to clear the runways of ice and snow. Unsophisticated? Maybe. Effective? One hundred percent!)

During the three-hour flight we had a pleasant meal, served by a bustling, motherly-looking matron—a far cry from the trim hostesses on American and European airlines. (Recently the Russian government has taken steps to remedy that situation!)

We landed in Moscow under chill, breezy skies. As yet there was no snow on the ground, but the weather was decidedly different from that of Paris. It was much like what we had just left in wintry Buenos Aires, except that there was no smog. Thank heaven for that.

Ralph Parker, a tall, friendly Englishman, met us. At customs we met Nina, who was to be our interpreter and constant companion for the entire trip. A trim-looking blonde, wearing a simple sweater and skirt, she could easily have been a typical American girl, found on any New York street. Nina was a distinct contrast to the average Russian woman, wearing her babushka.

Ralph Parker and Nina did all in their power to make us welcome. As we were whisked through customs without having our baggage inspected, we began to realize that we were going to get the red-carpet treatment for the whole trip.

At the Moscow airport we saw not a single plane of western design; nothing familiar was visible anywhere. I

remember the first time I set foot in Europe I was welcomed by advertisements for Firestone tires, Coca-Cola
and many other American products. The American influence was seen and felt everywhere—it was like bringing a little bit of home with you. Here in Moscow, I really
felt myself to be in a strange land, for the first time. Instead of the Ford Motor Company, it is Zim; instead of
Macy's, Gum Department Store; instead of Coca-Cola,
Fruit Water. No commercial advertisements appear on
billboards because there is no private enterprise to adver-
tise. As an equivalent, the Soviet government tacks slo-
gans on the face of every large building, bridge or arch-
way. "Communism is the people's government"; "Peace
to the world through Communism"; and hundreds of
other clichés penetrate your consciousness from every
direction, not in the wild profusion of western advertisements, but with consistent repetitiveness.

We were driven to a large, pre-revolutionary hotel,
filled with interesting old statues and urns; its rooms were
very large, in the old style. After settling ourselves in our
room and unpacking, we went down to the dining room
where we sat for a two-hour dinner. The food was nothing
special—notable only for the lack of vegetables and fruit.
Dessert was an extraordinary ice-cream dish, the like of
which I had never had. The Russians are great lovers of
ice cream, which, while singularly lacking in variety of
flavors, is rich and tasty.

The next morning my windpipe infection began to act
up again, probably aggravated by the long trip and lack
of sleep, and as we walked over to the Bolshoi Opera

House next morning I felt edgy because my voice was dull and scratchy from the infection.

Like La Scala at Milan and the old Metropolitan, the Bolshoi is unimpressive from the outside, but inside it is beautiful. Although its auditorium is much more intimate than the huge Met, its stage, by contrast, is enormous.

I was taken to a large room for my musical rehearsal with the staff and artists. At least twenty extra people had come to hear the new Boris from the U.S. My voice felt terrible and I was very self-conscious about my untried Russian. Instead of trying to use my voice I marked the part, which means I sang everything as softly as possible, oftentimes an octave below the written notes. When it became obvious that I was not going to use my voice many of the listeners began to leave. When the rehearsal was over I was told that I must go upstairs with the stage director and the rest of the cast for staging.

We wound our way up through a confusing maze of corridors to a large room on the top floor, where, with only a table, a chair and a few props we ran through the action. Toward the end, only the stage director, the pianist and the girl playing Feodor were left with Lucia and me. We then staged the famous death scene. As it progressed, I began to forget my self-consciousness about my Russian diction and began to live the part. As the scene came to a close I became aware that the stage director and the girl playing Feodor were both in tears.

Later Lucia said to me, "Did you see? You made them both cry during the death scene."

"Yes, I noticed, dear. Now I realize there is no language barrier. If my Russian is good enough to make them cry, it's good enough for the performance. Now let's patch up this voice of mine. Let's find a piano so I can vocalize."

When I vocalized my voice felt pretty good in spite of the infection. Then I was informed that my dress rehearsal was the next morning at 11:00 A.M. on stage. That worried me because it is hard to wake the voice up early, especially with a cold.

That night I slept fitfully, bothered by the time change. The next morning I arose early and began trying out my voice. My windpipe was worse. I felt a deep, unpleasant soreness, and when I took a deep breath I had to cough. A little black coffee helped, and I went right to the theater to make up and try on the costumes. (Russian artists are not allowed to make themselves up; each specialist does his own job, but as a guest I was allowed to do my own.) The staff looked at my wig and costumes disdainfully and commented that they were not Russian. I learned that this expression was used commonly for what was not pleasing to them. They got me one of their wigs and beards, and told me proudly that I was to be honored by being allowed to wear Chaliapin's costumes, since I was the same size he had been. The costumes had been in their opera museum for many years. I was indeed honored for Chaliapin was the great Russian bass, who brought *Boris* out of Russia for the first time in the early part of this century. He is the most adored singer ever to have trod Russian soil, despite the fact that he left the

Soviet Union because of his dislike for Communism and never returned to his homeland again.

They brought out his coronation costume and draped it on me. It was lined with two sets of heavy padding. I am six-foot-six-and-a-half and weigh 235 pounds, and in that costume I looked enormous. It must have weighed at least thirty-five pounds. I was thankful the coronation scene lasted only three minutes for me. Wearing it any longer while singing would have exhausted me.

I was determined not to use my voice during the rehearsal because Boris is dangerous even when the voice is healthy, and the famous mad scene of the second act calls for a terrific amount of emotion and shouting. Just as they called me to come on stage, the Lord said:

"Sing, Son. Use your voice."

I felt this much too risky, but the guidance persisted: *"Sing!"*

So I went on stage and did the first two acts full voice. After the second-act curtain the general manager and some of his staff crowded into my dressing room.

"What a pity," he said, "we will only have you for one performance. Can't you return after your tour and do a *Faust* for us too?"

"I would love to," I answered, "but I am supposed to go back to the Met for rehearsals on the sixteenth of October."

"With our schedule," he answered, "it would not be possible to do *Faust* until at least the twenty-second or twenty-third."

"That doesn't seem too likely a possibility," I said, "but I can try." I sent a telegram to Albert Gins, my lawyer, asking him to try to free me from the Met until at least the twenty-third.

By the time the rehearsal was over my voice felt very bad, and I asked the chief throat doctor in the theater to see if I had damaged my voice.

After a long examination the doctor picked up the phone, dialed a number and began to talk rapidly.

"What's he saying, Nina?" I asked.

My interpreter said, "He's talking to the director of the theater, and I think he's canceling you out of the performance."

"What?" I exclaimed. "He can't do that. The decision is mine."

"Things are quite different in the Soviet Union, Mr. Hines," said Nina. "It is the doctor's responsibility to decide whether or not you are well enough to sing, and he just told them to put someone else in the cast day after tomorrow in your place."

"Now, wait a minute. . . ." I got up out of my chair and said, "Nina, take me to the director immediately." I grabbed Lucia's arm and we walked briskly through the halls to the director's office.

"Nina said the doctor just canceled me out of the *Boris*."

"That's right, Mr. Hines; he says you cannot possibly sing Boris within the next two days."

"Well, that's what he says. I'll sing it. I have to."

"I'm sorry, Mr. Hines, but the doctor's word is law in the theater. It would be too dangerous for you to risk damaging your voice by singing Boris over a cold. You could harm your vocal cords seriously."

I stood there in confused silence. Finally I countered with, "Look, could we postpone the performance for a couple of days?"

"That would mean canceling a performance in Leningrad. We would have to call and see if this is possible. But if you could return and sing on the twenty-third of October the problem would be solved."

"I'm afraid that's impossible," I said. "It'll have to be next week."

A call to the government agency of Goz Koncert did not help. They insisted that Leningrad could not be canceled—even one performance—and that if I could not sing my scheduled performance, I would have to forego a Moscow appearance.

"Well, Mr. Hines," said the director, "I am afraid you are out of luck. Leningrad cannot be canceled, and you most likely cannot remain after your tour. It is a pity— we had looked forward to your performance, especially after such an excellent dress rehearsal."

"Then I'll sing the day after tomorrow."

"The doctor says, 'No,' Mr. Hines," sighed the director.

"Look, do you expect me to come all the way to Moscow from the United States just to tour the Soviet Union? Without singing at the Bolshoi? I've got to sing."

The director looked at me a long time, then said, "Mr.

Hines, I know exactly how you feel; I was a leading tenor in this theater for almost thirty years. All right, I am going to make an exception in your case—you may make the decision, not the doctor. But I must know your decision tomorrow morning, for sure. And remember, Mr. Hines, if you tell me you are going to sing, no one will be around to substitute for you at the last moment. You will have to sing."

"I'll let you know tomorrow," I said bleakly and left, with a concerned Lucia and Nina trailing behind.

When we got to the hotel room Lucia said, "Darling, don't sing if you think you are going to hurt yourself. Oh what terrible situation. Moscow ees so important. . . . But you must decide. Don' let me influence you."

Ralph Parker called, concerned about how I felt, and also to let me know he had arranged a press conference for the next day.

"All of the American press will be there, the Russian press too. It's a rather important moment. Deucedly unpleasant time to get sick. I sympathize with you. How do you feel about it?"

"I'll decide in the morning and let you know immediately," I said. Lucia and I ate a gloomy dinner, which was interrupted by a tall, young man who introduced himself as a fellow-American who had just arrived from New York. After dessert, as I excused myself, the young chap offered us a copy of *The New York Times*.

"Revolution Breaks Out in Argentina" leaped out of the *Times* headlines. The article said that jets were bombing Buenos Aires and that the international airport had been closed.

"Good heavens, Lucia, if we had stayed a little longer we would never have gotten out in time to arrive in Moscow. Let's see, what's the date of this paper?" It was dated the morning after we had left Buenos Aires.

"Well," I said pensively, "the circle of protection promised by the Lord seems to be in effect all right—the revolutions started hours after we left!"

I spent another near-sleepless night, and when I dragged myself out of bed the next morning, I couldn't even speak. We went downstairs for breakfast and I sat as silent as a zombie.

"How can you possibly sing tomorrow?" my wife asked. "You can't even talk. What are you going to do? You have to tell the theater this morning."

"I'm going to take a walk," I croaked and walked out into the damp, hazy Moscow morning. It was drizzling slightly as I wandered around the Kremlin into the Red Square.

"God, what are you trying to do to me? Did you bring me all the way to Russia just to ruin me? The whole world will be watching my performance and I can't even talk."

I ranted on at the Lord for the better part of an hour and finally returned to the hotel no better off than when I had left. Lucia was waiting in the lobby.

"What have you decide?"

"I don't know," I groaned.

"We must go to the theater."

"I know, I know. I'm going upstairs a moment. Wait here."

I went up to our room agonized in the spirit.

"Oh, God," I cried, "what shall I do. Please—what shall I do?"

"Open your Bible," was the response.

I picked it up off of the night table, flipped it open and read from II Timothy: ". . . therefore endure hardness as a good soldier of Jesus Christ."

"Well," I said, "now what does that mean?"

"Son," said that inner voice, *"I am not asking you to sing tomorrow."*

Momentarily I drew a sigh of relief until. . . .

"No, I am not asking you to sing, I am ordering you to sing. I have not brought you all the way to Moscow just to have you foul up the whole affair. I brought you here for a purpose. Now sing."

Hotly, I shot back, "Well, if the devil couldn't touch me for two months, how come I got sick?"

"You are now in the extraordinary position of being able to see what is the devil's responsibility and what is your own. You are not sick because the devil struck you down; you are sick because you were so afraid of singing in Moscow that you brought this on yourself. Now pick yourself up like a man and sing."

I needed no more. I put on my coat and ran down the stairs to Lucia.

"Let's go," I said firmly. She took courage by what she saw on my face. We hastened over to the theater and were quickly brought to the director.

"I'm going to sing tomorrow," I told the director firmly.

"Bravo. Good for you," he said. "I'm glad."

"Now get me to a good doctor and let's do what we can for this throat."

A kindly, sympathetic woman doctor examined my throat and said in Russian, "According to the report I received from the theater doctor, you must be much improved. I think there is a good chance you might be able to sing if your cords improve some more."

"By the way, Mr. Hines, you are a most unusual man," she continued, through my interpreter.

"How so?"

"Well, all of the Bolshoi singers who come in here with something wrong with their throats, crawl in the door looking miserable—practically in tears. You are different—completely different. You have such a wonderful spirit about you. How do you explain that?"

Not trusting my interpreter to be accurate enough to pass on my words, I said directly in Russian:

"Ya Christyaian. Ya znayu moy bog." ("I am a Christian. I know my God.")

The smirk Nina tossed the doctor was replaced quickly by surprise when the doctor said, "Most of the artists at the Bolshoi are believers. And that is very important. Well, when you come again tomorrow I hope you will be much improved."

The next morning I arose and tried to make some sound, but I still could hardly speak. Again I wandered the streets of Moscow, but I could find no solace, no help from the Lord. When I finally arrived back at the corner by my hotel I stopped and said, "Lord, you got me into this, so it must be your will that I do it. Please help."

"It is my will that you sing today. Now make it your will too."

I had often prayed, "Lord, Thy will is my will." I had always felt that my will was something to be discarded, so God's will could be used instead. Then I always went along reluctantly with God—dragging my heels, so to speak. Now I realized I had used the wrong inflection in that sentence; it should go: "Thy will is my *will*." I made up my mind and said, "All right, Lord. I *will* sing tonight." In the following few moments of guidance I came to realize that the reason I was to fast once a week was to help me build a spiritual discipline and to temper my will so it would be strong enough to respond to the arduous task that lay ahead.

Early in the afternoon I vocalized and my voice began to respond. I went to the theater two and one-half hours before curtain time and began the long makeup job. By curtain time my voice felt reasonably secure. Soon the dark, stirring chorus of the first scene began and I got into the coronation costume. I was escorted to the stage amid anxious inquiries about the condition of my voice from my Russian colleagues. Their genuine concern for me was quite touching, and was my first taste of the warmth and generosity of the Russian people.

I got in my place for the coronation procession. Great ten-ton steeple chimes, mounted permanently on the rear wall of the stage, began to peal loudly, and I entered. What a beautiful sight the Bolshoi Opera House is from

the stage. I walked forward on the immense stage to
the accompaniment of the enormous chorus singing,
"Slava! Slava!" ("Glory! Glory!") to the Czar Boris. The
chorus threw roses by the hundreds in my path as I
walked slowly down the long ramp to the footlights. Then
came the great hush before Boris sings, "My Soul is Sad"—
the hush of a terrible premonition as the fear of God's
retribution for his crime strikes him.

My voice felt steady and fairly clear. I sang the short
but difficult pages cautiously, then it was over. Back in
my dressing room after the curtain calls I changed into
my costume for the second act hastily—this was the tough
one. If I gave too much I would not have enough voice
left for the lyric death scene at the end. If I gave too little,
the mad scene in the second act would be lifeless.

As I began the second act I could see Lucia sitting in
the box nearest the stage; her presence helped. I seemed
to do reasonably well, and there was good applause after
the second act—nothing special though. I returned to the
dressing room to wait for Lucia and her impression.

She came in with a strange look on her face.

"How was it?" I asked.

"Fine," she answered. But something about her manner
bothered me.

"Lo dici male," I said. ("You say it badly.") "Come
on, tell me the truth."

"I'll tell you after."

"No, tell me now!" I insisted.

"Can't you give a little more voice?"

"That's all I have to give," I said.

"It's not enough. It doesn't sound like you. It doesn't have that rich flowing sound. It just isn't enough. You've got to give more."

"I'll try."

I went to the piano and vocalized some more, but my voice went entirely rough. Just then they called me onstage for the scene in which Boris meets the village idiot who accuses him publicly of his crime. I had only three or four little lines to sing, but when I got onstage I could hardly muster enough voice to sing even those few words. Panic gripped me. How could I get through the death scene? Would I have to stop in the middle and walk offstage? I had no voice left. I walked numbly back to my dressing room and sat staring in the mirror.

"God, God, where are you?" He seemed infinitely distant and I felt terribly alone. All too soon I was called to the stage for the death scene. Before leaving the dressing room I tried a couple of scales. My voice wouldn't respond. But there was no escape. As I stood in the wings I could see various newsmen waiting for my entrance with their cameras.

"Waiting for my disaster," I thought blackly.

In a spasm of anguish, I cried out in my heart, "God! Oh God! Kill me! I want to die! I have failed you. Failed you completely. You've brought me all the way to Moscow just to have me ruin everything. I want to die. Kill me!"

Then it was my cue to go onstage. I turned and walked before the audience to the clicking and whirring of movie cameras from the wings.

11.

Go in My Name

THE DEATH scene was the most important. I had been secretly planning an innovation at the end of it—a way to get across a little Christian witness to the Russian public. Afraid that I wouldn't be permitted to do it, I had not tried it in the dress rehearsal.

(In the opera, Boris suffers from the terrible guilt of having murdered the child, Dimitri, in order to attain the throne in his stead. Throughout the story Boris implores God vainly to forgive him for his crime and is slowly going insane from his guilt. At the end of the opera his last words are, "God, I am dying. . . . Forgive me. Forgive me." Then he falls down the stairs from his throne. The music that follows is so ethereal and peaceful that one knows that Boris has found peace with God in death.)

I intended to strengthen this idea by adding a few extra words of my own (in Russian of course). As I cried out, "Forgive me," I was going to gasp, then smile, as if held by an ethereal vision, and say, *"Oh Moi Boje. . . . Blagadaryou vas."* ("Oh, my God. . . . Thank you.")

I wish I could say that I had prayed a beautiful prayer of faith backstage, and had felt a wonderful surge of heavenly power, and sang like an angel with no problems. But it just wasn't so. My prayer was one of utter despair.

I went onstage for the last scene like a sore, wounded soldier, fighting for his very life. Every note seemed like my last. I hung on and fought savagely—it was the worst struggle I ever had on any stage. Under normal circumstances I would never have gone on in such a condition, but these were not normal circumstances.

My long, strenuous training in the language and the role paid off. Although my voice balked and my mind was foggy, the words and actions flowed smoothly and instinctively, and I was able to concentrate on my singing. After what seemed an eternity, I climbed the steps to the throne, crying out, "I still am the Czar!" Then, "Oh God, I'm dying."

Only a couple of lines to gasp out and it would be over. "Forgive me. Forgive—me."

Would it be too offensive to the Communists to tack a real Christian ending onto the greatest of all Russian operas? Should I do it, or just leave well enough alone? These thoughts raced through my mind; the inner voice said, "Do it."

I did. Then I paused dramatically and plunged to the floor with a crash. I was dimly aware that the public was cheering and yelling, interrupting the minute-long postlude before the curtain fell.

My colleagues ran over and helped me to my feet, asking the usual queries—had I hurt myself in the fall?

The rest of the cast pushed me out on the stage to

face the audience alone. I was almost in a state of shock from the strain of the last act.

The audience rose to its feet in a standing ovation and began the typical Russian expression of clapping in unison as they do when they like something especially well.

I returned to the wings and pulled my colleagues out with me. The soprano handed me a bouquet of flowers and I kissed her on the cheek. The Russians, seeing an American kiss one of their own onstage, went wild. At long last the curtain calls ended. I was still not sure what had happened until Lucia ran backstage and threw her arms about me.

"Oh, Darling, that was the greatest death scene you've ever done in your life."

I took her under my arm, wiped the tears from her eyes, and waded through the crowd toward the dressing room. Countless times we were stopped by well-wishers and newsmen. Finally, I got into the dressing room and wearily removed my costume and makeup. I was half out on my feet.

We were taken to a reception held in honor of the conductor, Melik Pashayev, and myself. When I was brought over to the conductor I asked him pointedly, "What did you think of my innovation at the end of the opera?"

Everyone stopped to listen to his answer, and Pashayev was well aware of it. He replied carefully but meaningfully: "I think it was in perfect accord with the composer's wishes."

I could not have received a more satisfying answer.

The next morning we were up at 6:30 to catch a plane to Leningrad. Now the real solid work was to begin. During the next seven days I would have to rehearse and do two performances in *Boris* and one in *Faust*. That meant, including the night before, four performances in eight days. Ordinarily that would be a two-week job.

As Lucia, Nina and I walked through a pouring rain to board our jet, I wondered how I could possibly sing such a schedule. Right now I could barely speak above a hoarse whisper.

We took our seats on the plane and Nina said, "Mr. Hines, when we arrive in Leningrad this afternoon you can rest the remainder of the day. Tomorrow is your dress rehearsal for Boris and the following day you sing it."

I winced at that.

"You know," I said to the girls, "if I could just sing *Faust* first, instead of *Boris* I think I could make it."

"But Jerry," Lucia said staring, *"Faust* is so much singing. *Boris* is shorter."

"I know, but *Faust* is very cantabile. It's the yelling and emotion in *Boris* that will hurt my voice."

Nina said matter-of-factly, "Well, there's no way to change it now, I suppose."

"I suppose not," I sighed and settled back for the take-off. After we were in the air I said inwardly, "Lord, how can I sing such a schedule for the rest of the tour?"

"Son, you must tackle your problems one at a time. You concentrate on your next performance as if it were the

only one you had to do. You cannot sing them all at once. You attend to the immediate performance and trust me to prepare everything else. Don't save yourself. Do your very best."

In *Boris,* I thought wryly, my best won't be much two days from now.

News of the Moscow success had preceded me to Leningrad, and my colleagues at the Kirov Theater met me with enthusiasm.

I arrived early the next morning for a staging rehearsal of *Boris.* The dress rehearsal with orchestra was set for the afternoon. The conductor welcomed me into his office eagerly.

"Mr. Hines," he began, through my interpreter, "now do we understand clearly? You do sing the Shostakovich version of *Boris* as well as the Rimsky-Korsakov version that you did at the Bolshoi?"

"Oh, yes," I replied, "as I notified you previously, we do the Shostakovich version at the Met." (This version follows closely the original ideas of the old Moussorgsky score and is quite different musically from the Rimsky-Korsakov revision, which is used almost the world over.)

"But Mr. Hines," he persisted, "are you aware that there are *two* Shostakovich versions? The early one that he did many years ago is the one we perform."

A little alarm bell began to ring in my mind. The score they had sent me months before had contained the second act in two versions, one of which I had never seen before—it looked as if it came from an entirely different opera. The other version was the one which Shostakovich had reorchestrated and which we performed currently at the Met.

My heart sank as he opened the score to the version I didn't know.

"This is the version Shostakovich originally orchestrated—the one we do here."

"I'm sorry, but that was not made clear in your letter and I don't know it."

There was a hurried consultation with the staff and an attempt was made to call Moscow to see if the orchestral parts could be sent out, and some singers too, who could do the Rimsky-Korsakov version.

"No matter what finally happens," said the conductor, "we must switch the opera for tomorrow to *Faust.*"

I stared in open-mouthed amazement. My wish was coming true—what a stroke of luck! My thoughts flashed to that "circle of protection," and to the day before: *"You attend to the immediate performance and trust me to prepare everything else."*

The Lord's hand in my affairs was becoming more obvious; I began to cheer up and take hope.

The arrangements were completed swiftly, and we rehearsed the *Faust* all day. As in Moscow, my colleagues were warm and friendly and brought Lucia and me souvenirs or flowers. It was the same in every theater: We met with a certain reserve and aloofness at first, until I made a few friendly gestures in rehearsal. At the first show of kindness, everybody fell all over themselves to be friendly. The Russian people are easy to love.

I had sung *Faust* in French since I was twenty years old, and by late afternoon my voice felt much clearer. It was a good feeling to be back on familiar ground—a bit distracting to have all my cues sung at me in Russian, but I soon got used to that. By the day of the performance my voice began to feel like its old self again, and I was feeling much more assured. Lucia was nervous as could be, but she tried to hide it from me. I believe I sang the best *Faust* of my life that night. After the first act Lucia came running to the dressing room almost hysterically happy, tears streaming down her face.

"You sound like two basses instead of one," she sobbed happily.

After the "Calf of Gold" aria in the first act even the chorus applauded onstage, and when I finally came offstage, all of them were standing in the wings cheering so loudly that it struck me funny. I motioned for them to stop a moment and when they did I called out in Russian, "Praise God, not me."

There was a surprised silence and then a cheer went up twice as loud as the previous one. There was a jubilant air to the whole performance, and it came to a grand successful close.

The next morning I was greeted by the news that it would be impossible to put a Rimsky-Korsakov *Boris* together in time. So we would repeat *Faust* the next

day, and then two days after that do *The Barber of
Seville*.

Great! The part of the singing teacher, Don Basilio,
was one of the real fun-parts in opera. Also it's not taxing
on the voice at all. I was elated with my good fortune
and thanked the good Lord promptly.

The next day was free so Lucia and I took a tour of
Leningrad. What a beautiful city it is. Truly it is of the
stature of Paris or Rome. We drank in as many of the
wonderful sights as we could. Of course, we were told
that this bridge was the most beautiful in the world, that
building the finest of its type, etc.

At St. Isaac's Cathedral, which is truly gorgeous, Nina
said, "I suppose this cathedral is much bigger than St.
Peter's in Rome."

Lucia's Italian honor had been assaulted to its limit.

"My dear," she said condescendingly. "You could put
three of these in Saint Peter's."

And Lucia strode off, completely satisfied with Nina's
expression of surprise and consternation. We went outside.

"Who did you say built this monument?" asked Lucia,
pointing to a beautiful structure on the left.

"A famous Russian," said Nina.

"What was the name again?" Lucia pursued, eyes flash-
ing. Hearing Nina's reply, Lucia snapped, "That's an Italian name."

"Well, he did come from Italy, but he eventually became a Russian citizen and spent the rest of his life here."

"Aha!" said Lucia pertly. Now her Italian honor had been properly restituted.

We went partway across the city by bus, and then got off and walked. I stopped and looked at what seemed to be a large cathedral on the right.

"Oh, that's the Kazansky Cathedral," said Nina. This I had heard of, and I wanted to go in.

"Well, it's not a cathedral anymore," she added too hastily. "It's a museum now."

"I know," I said, persisting. "I want to see it."

"But it's a museum of religion and atheism," she said uncomfortably.

"I know, Nina, but I—want—to—see it!"

Nina turned to Lucia with a hint of anxiety, "It's getting late. We'd better go back to the hotel."

Lucia frowned thoughtfully, "Why, Nina? We have nothing to do tonight. What's the hurry? Come on, let's go in."

Lucia and I led the way, with Nina dragging her heels. My blood ran cold as we entered and looked about. I had heard of this place but I did not expect what I saw. Every man has a right to believe or not to believe in God, but this was too much. This beautiful cathedral had been desecrated by literally hundreds of exhibits—all anti-religious in character and particularly anti-Christian.

I paused before a large, gory oil painting. The scene was the interior of a simple wood-frame house. A man stood in the middle of it with a bloody axe in his hand. On the bed in front of him lay the butchered body of a woman. Underneath the painting was a long printed explanation. It was too much for my limited Russian vocabulary.

"Nina, read the explanation to me, please," I said coolly.

"It's very long, Mr. Hines."

"I have plenty of time. Read it, Nina."

I don't remember the exact words but the story behind the picture was that a man, a Baptist living in a rural area, had discovered that his wife had been taking instructions secretly to become a Communist—he had hacked her to death in her sleep with an axe. This was considered a demonstration of the extremes of fanaticism to which organized religions could drive human beings.

We walked on to the next exhibit and the next—more of the same. I don't know if Nina was trying to avoid awkward situations because she was supposed to, as a good interpreter, or if she was embarrassed by the museum's harsh message.

A man has a right to choose to not believe in God if he wishes, but I'd like to suggest to the Soviet Union that if it wishes to convince the world that there is no pressure on believers under Communism it might do well to remove some of the Stalinist hangovers like the desecration of the Kazansky Cathedral.

The week drew to a close with a lively and extremely funny version of *The Barber of Seville*. It was a great personal satisfaction to have a four-minute applause after my main aria, "La Calunnia." The theater has never allowed encores. (When I returned to Leningrad three years later in 1965 I broke that tradition by repeating

Mefistofele's serenade during my first *Faust* of that season.)

At the end of this stimulating week I received a query from Moscow, asking if I could stay a week beyond my projected tour to perform in Riga and Minsk. With it came the news that the Met had released me so I could return for another performance at the Bolshoi. I could return and do *Faust* on the twenty-third of October.

We left Leningrad with fond memories and flew to the Ukraine. There, in Kiev, I sang two *Fausts* and a *Boris*, but here the task became harder because encores were permitted and in the *Faust* performances I had to repeat both arias. Although I was doing well vocally, it was very strenuous and by the end of the week my voice was seriously tired. As we were preparing to leave Kiev, the administrator of the theater, who had been especially kind to us, said, "Thank God you're going."

"Why, Arnold?" I asked, surprised. The week long he had been a model of good manners.

"Alas," he said, "I have lost all of my friends because of you. They all wanted tickets and I had none. Six hundred extra people beyond the theater's capacity crowded your *Boris*. The conservatory students who couldn't get in started a riot and we had to call the police."

"I had a man practically sitting in my lap half of the performance," Lucia laughed. "And you couldn't find the aisles, people were packed in so tightly."

Arnold wished us Godspeed and a quick return to Kiev, and again we took off for new adventure in Tblisi, the capital of Georgia. My windpipe infection now seemed almost entirely gone, but I was so tired vocally that I was hardly able to speak. I said to the girls, "I don't know how much longer I can take this pace."

"But Mr. Hines," said Nina, "You only have two performances this week."

"Yes," I countered, "but my voice is dead-tired and we start off with *Boris* again. I wish it could be switched so I could do *Faust* first, as I did in Leningrad."

At Tblisi we were met by the sweet-faced, white-haired director of the theater. On the way to the car he said, "Mr. Hines, I hope you don't mind, but I took the liberty of switching your performances around. I thought it would be better psychology for the public to hear your *Faust* first, then *Boris*."

Nina and Lucia looked at me as if I were some kind of a sacred cow. It was eerie how everything seemed to be going my way.

In spite of my fatigue, the two performances went extraordinarily well. *Boris* was so successful I had a half-hour of curtain calls after the performance. Emboldened by this and knowing that Tblisi had a reputation for still being a very religious city, on impulse I made the sign of the orthodox cross to the audience on my last curtain call. The few hundred people left in the auditorium almost stopped applauding for a moment. Then about a third of them began applauding again and another third began hissing me from all directions. That was the final curtain call for sure!

During the previous week, both Lucia and Nina had come down with my cold. I don't know whether I was reinfected by them or had a relapse because of the strain, but I woke up the morning after *Boris* with a bad throat again. The weather was bad and there was not always sufficient heat.

My next performance was three days off, in Riga. At breakfast, when I complained of my relapse, Nina pointed out that I had two days' rest.

"If I just had one more day's rest," I said, "I think I could make it."

This is starting to sound absurd but—it happened again! Within an hour Nina received a telegram from Moscow: The Riga and Minsk performances had both been postponed by one day. That was not the only good news— the Bolshoi had decided to make my return performance another *Boris* instead of *Faust,* because of the previous success.

Now my joy was complete. That night as I lay in bed thinking aout the fantastic results of the tour I grew increasingly excited. I realized that the Lord had indeed put a fabulous circle of protection around us—witness the great success in Moscow in spite of me dragging my heels in disbelief.

"Oh God," I cried out in my heart, "you have kept every promise so wonderfully well, and I have acted so miserably."

Another thought began to form in my mind. "Lord," I began, "do your servant just one more favor. Give me Khrushchev at my return performance at the Bolshoi. That would be the unbelievable part, the most wonderful."

*"Ask in faith. Just as you walked in faith when I took
you to your wife in Buenos Aires, ask in faith."*

But this seemed so impossible I hardly dared believe
it. The next day I spoke with Parker on the phone. Still
thinking about Khrushchev I decided to help the Lord a
bit, and asked Parker if he could do anything to try to
get the Premier to come.

"If he didn't come to the first performance, he'll never
come to the second," he answered. "It's not even worth
trying."

But each night for the remainder of the trip I kept
asking the Lord, "Please give me Khrushchev at my performance."

The answer always was, *"Ask in faith."*

We returned to Moscow three days before the performance. Bill Jones was there waiting for me. A year before
he had promised to meet me in Moscow to film my visit
there. He took me to the Moscow Baptist Church where
I sang, as he took pictures for his Presidential Prayer
Breakfast films. He then asked if I could get permission
for him to film my performance at the Bolshoi, from the
electrician's box in the middle of the stage. I agreed to try,
and the Bolshoi management cooperated.

The night before the performance Bill Jones said to
Lucia and me at supper, "You know, I have a funny feeling that something big is going to happen tomorrow night
at the Bolshoi." I thought of Khrushchev, but held my
peace.

The next morning at breakfast, Bill announced, "I just
heard a rumor that President Kennedy announced a block-

ade of Cuba last night, and they'll be stopping any Russian ships that try to run the blockade. This could mean war."

The rumor was confirmed while Lucia, Bill and I were having lunch with American Ambassador Foy Kohler. I began to wonder how my audience was going to react at the evening performance. *Now* where was that circle of protection? I was surely going to need it to face a hostile audience, especially if the blockade were announced to the Russian public before curtain time. Sure enough it was announced publicly just about an hour and a half before the performance began. What a situation!

Bill arrived soon after that and began to set up his cameras. Lucia arrived looking very beautiful in an emerald-green evening gown. She had not worn it once for the entire trip, because no one dressed formally for the opera and she would have looked out of place, but tonight Nina had insisted she wear it for this last performance. She looked like a dream.

She too was concerned about the public's reaction to the political situation and felt that our departure for New York next morning would be none too soon. Just then Bill broke into the dressing room.

"Hey, Jerry, I've just been kicked offstage with my cameras."

"Why?" I said, startled.

"Khrushchev's coming!"

I stood there looking at Bill, with my mouth gaping open.

"I have to take the films from the wings," he went on

excitedly. "Boy, if I could just get a picture of him. But they won't hear of it."

"What a God we've got. What a God we've got," I kept saying over and over. Then I realized that Khrushchev had come to the performance as a political move.

"Ask in faith," the Lord had said.

Lucia finally went to her box and I got into Chaliapin's coronation costume again. The music began and I went to the stage to seek Bill. I found him amidst a tangle of cameras and tripods he had set up in the wings.

"Let's have a word of prayer, Bill." He and I must have made an incongruous sight: Bill Jones, technical book publisher loaded with cameras and Jerry Hines dressed in Chaliapin's Boris costume—two Californians standing in the wings of the Bolshoi, heads bowed amid the confusion of pre-performance, praying to our Lord and God, Jesus Christ. And all this only a few feet away from Premier Khrushchev, sitting in his box!

I took my place in line for the coronational procession, closed my eyes and said, "Lord, give me your blessing."

"Go in my name," was the short reply. I opened my eyes and stared into the face of Jesus Christ. A supernumerary was standing in front of me holding a banner showing the head of Christ with a crown of thorns emblazoned on it. He led the way and I followed.

I have never known such a moment: The cries of "Glory to Boris" rang in my ears as I walked forward to perform for the rulers of the Communist world, and I walked in the sure knowledge that I was there as an emissary of Jesus Christ.

12.

Fulfillment

IN A FEW MINUTES the short scene of the coronation was over. I walked out for my curtain call and the audience, to a man, rose to their feet in a standing ovation. I couldn't understand what was happening. I looked into the royal box in the rear center hoping to catch a glimpse of Khrushchev—the box was full, but I couldn't distinguish his familiar figure.

After I returned to my dressing room, Lucia dashed in, crying, "Darling, what you trying to do, insult Mr. Khrushchev? He stood up and motion for the public to give you thees standing ovation and you don' even geev heem a bow. Nothing!"

"Honey, I looked for him, but I couldn't see him."

"Couldn't see heem. Ees almost seeting in your lap, in the box right by the stage."

"Which side?" I asked.

"On the left."

"All right, calm down, I'll give him a good acknowledgment after the second act."

"If he's still there," came the voice of Ralph Parker. "He never stays more than an act or two. Remember he's a very sick man."

"Well, I hope he stays for this. I don't want him to think I was snubbing him deliberately."

Then I was back onstage again. I looked into the box on the left, and my heart sank in dismay—a lone woman sat there. The others had left. Disappointed, I finished the scene, took my curtain calls and returned to the dressing room.

The door burst open. "Jerrrry, what you try to do, start World War III?" Lucia was wildly excited. "Everybody in the opera has a bow to Khrushchev. You want him to go home mad an' pusha de button, an' poof, no more world?"

"Honey, I looked in the box. He wasn't there."

"What box? On the left? The box ona *my* left, you crazy man."

"Oh, no!" I grabbed my head. "You mean I was looking at the wrong box? He's still there? Now he must be sure I'm snubbing him because, as an American, I'm mad over Cuba."

I summoned the stage director.

"Please send someone to Premier Khrushchev's box to tell him that it is an oversight that I have not acknowledged his presence and that if he'll stay to the end of the opera I will do it without fail."

She backed off, wide-eyed. "Oh, no."

No amount of persuasion could change her mind—she was not about to get involved. She kept insisting he would stay to the end, but I wasn't as sure as she.

Again I went on stage. After the village idiot scene there was only an open tableau, no curtain calls. I kept praying that he would stay to the end. Finally the opera was over and I came out for my curtain call. Again the audience was on its feet. I looked at the right-hand box and there was the familiar figure applauding vigorously.

I walked across the stage to the box; when I was only about six feet from the Premier I made a low, dramatic bow and then returned to the center. (Lucia later commented that she thought I was going to shake hands with him.)

When the applause finally died down I was told that Premier Khrushchev was waiting for my wife and me. Still in costume and makeup, I, along with Nina, was ushered into a large room replete with refreshments and about thirty men—most of the big brass of Moscow, including Khrushchev, Mikoyan and the President of the Rumanian Republic.

Immediately after I was introduced to the Premier, a toast was proposed to my performance. I stopped the proceedings by saying that I liked to share all the important things in life with my wife—would they hold up the toast until she arrived? Someone was dispatched to find her, and she arrived breathlessly a few moments later.

When I heard her say, "Oh Mr. Khrushchev, thees the most exciting moment of my life," I winced. Taking her aside I whispered, "You said the same thing to President Kennedy."

"Be quiet, I know what I am doing," she answered saucily.

"My but you are tall," said Khrushchev—I towered over him by a good fourteen inches.

"I want to warn you, Mr. Khrushchev, I am a California midget." (Now the reader knows why Russia really backed down on the Cuban crisis!) Everyone laughed.

"That fall you took at the end seems very dangerous. Where did you learn to do that?" he asked.

"I took tumbling in college."

"Hmm." Khrushchev turned to his right. "Mikoyan, do you think you could learn to take a fall like that without hurting yourself?" Mikoyan looked perplexed.

"No, you'd better not try, you are too important to affairs of state." The conversation was light and casual for a while, until the Premier asked me about Russian music and art in America.

"Is it popular?"

"Why yes," I answered. "Russian music is very popular. We still have fond memories of Feodor Chaliapin. His bust now stands in the lobby of the Met."

Khrushchev's face reddened, as he told me that Feodor Chaliapin was a stupid man and failed to understand Communism in its true light. Other artists were more intelligent than he and remained in the Soviet Union to perform and produce under Communism. In the city where he [Khrushchev] was living during the revolution a group of artists hid in the home of a woman, waiting for their chance to escape from the Soviet Union. But fortunately, this woman happened to speak with some Communists, and they convinced her that the real future for the arts lay in Communism. So she went back home to the artists who were hiding there and pleaded with them for a long time until she convinced them they should go back to their homes and serve their arts under Communism. "And today that city exports the greatest artists to the entire world," Khrushchev concluded.

He picked up his glass and, since every conversation seemed to end in a toast, I was sure that we would now have a toast to the Russian Revolution, which would put me in an embarrassing position. How could I, as an American, drink a toast to the Communist Revolution? Khrushchev must have seen the look on my face because he stopped, glass poised in mid-air and drily added that all he'd said was "just propaganda."

There was a big laugh all around and I was much relieved. The subject changed to pleasantries such as, "Where did you learn such good Russian diction?" etc. Finally, after about half an hour had passed, Khrushchev raised his glass significantly, looked directly and meaningfully at me, and proposed a toast to "peace and friendship between our countries."

"I'll drink to that," I said clearly. After the toast I said to the Premier in my best Russian, *"Blagaslavi Vas Bog."* ("God bless you.") Khrushchev looked as if he were about to say, "This to me?" And all laughed again. The reception was over.

As we left, Lucia and I still didn't completely realize the full import of the situation. We were a small part of one of the great climaxes of history. Khrushchev's action that night in determining to take a step of appeasement on Cuba was the very beginning of the great split between Russia and China. It was the beginning of the end for Khrushchev's political career. In a sense, he had also come to the Bolshoi to make my wife and me unofficial ambassadors to go back to the West bearing the news that there would be no war over Cuba. He knew we were returning to New York the next day and he refused to see the American ambassador or any representatives from the West in the ensuing days. Only Lucia and I had any inkling of what the outcome would be.

When we arrived in New York the next evening the airport was swarming with reporters and interviewers. The one question on everybody's mind was, "Will there be war tomorrow when we stop the first Russian ship?" The whole world was holding its breath. Lucia and I were the only two people outside of the Kremlin who had a ray of hope.

Our family was waiting at the airport for us also, but we had to spend two hours there just doing interviews. It was late that night when we climbed gratefully into our beds—back home again after a long and amazing journey.

A couple of days later I was looking at the flood of news clippings that came in from all over the world. I still could hardly believe all this had happened to me. Then I thought back to that conversation with the Lord at Seaside Park two months before.

"Payment in full will come in Moscow. I have prepared something for you there that will be so stupendous, so fantastic, that when it happens you will not be able to believe it."

The circle of protection was completed too: We had just read in the paper that anti-American demonstrators had begun stoning Ambassador Foy Kohler's car at the time we were taking off from Moscow. Like the Argentina revolution, we had missed it by a hair.

Lucia walked into the room. Looking at all the clippings she said, "Some publicity."

And to think that I was going to pull a cheap, faked publicity stunt in *Boris* nine years before! I thought of Eisenhower, Kennedy and finally Khrushchev, and realized the full import of the rest of that passage in Psalm 113:

> Who is like unto the Lord our God, who dwelleth
> on high,
> Who humbleth himself to behold the things that
> are in heaven, and in the earth!
> He raiseth up the poor out of the dust, and lift-
> eth the needy out of the dunghill;
> That he may set him with princes, even with
> the princes of his people.
> He maketh the barren woman to keep house, and
> to be a joyful mother of children. Praise ye the
> Lord.

Only a few days afterward Lucia announced to me that we had conceived our fourth child in Russia.

In a period of less than ten years I can say that I, in spite of a skeptical scientifically trained mind, came to recognize Jesus Christ as Saviour, actually experiencing the joy of direct communication with Him. I found that miracles exist and that God is a personal God who cares for the individual—in fact, He cared enough to die for me.

Truly this book began as my story, but it has ended another way.

> *This is my story, this is my song,*
> *Praising my Saviour all the day long.*